# Duino Elegies

AND

# The Sonnets to Orpheus

# Duino Elegies

## AND

# The Sonnets to Orpheus

# Rainer Maria Rilke

EDITED AND TRANSLATED BY

*Stephen Mitchell*

*Vintage International*
VINTAGE BOOKS
A DIVISION OF RANDOM HOUSE, INC.
NEW YORK

Library of Congress Cataloging-in-Publication Data:

Rilke, Rainer Maria, 1875–1926.
[Duineser Elegien. English]
Duino elegies ; and, The sonnets to Orpheus / Rainer Maria Rilke ; edited and
translated by Stephen Mitchell. —1st Vintage International ed.
p. cm.
ISBN 978-0-307-47373-8
1. Rilke, Rainer Maria, 1875–1926—Translations into English.   2. Elegiac poetry,
German—Translations into English.   3. Sonnets, German—Translations into
English.   4. German poetry—Translations into English.   I. Mitchell, Stephen,
1943–   II. Rilke, Rainer Maria, 1875–1926. Sonette an Orpheus. English.
III. Title.   IV. Title: Sonnets to Orpheus.
PT2635.I65D813   2009
831.912—dc22
2009021983

This symbol, *, indicates a space between sections of a poem whenever such spaces are lost in pagination.

# Contents

SECOND PART

## APPENDIX TO THE SONNETS TO ORPHEUS

# Foreword

The *Duino Elegies* are widely acknowledged to be the greatest poem of the twentieth century; *The Sonnets to Orpheus*, in their subtler way (string quartets to the *Elegies'* full orchestra), are at least as great. Is it possible to speak of them and not speak in superlatives? "I have always found the *Elegies* hard to compare or even read with our own best poems," Robert Lowell once said.

Entire books have been written about each of these masterpieces. My job here is to write a brief foreword telling the story of their composition. The most useful place to begin is with the angel of the *Elegies*.

Rilke wrote about angels all his life. His earlier angels are lovely: supple-meaninged and light-winged, as even the most graceful Leonardo or Raphael angel can't be, since, rather than in the gravitas of paint, these angels are embodied in the invisible element of words. The most charming of the early angels is the speaker in a poem called "Annunciation" (it is Gabriel, of course, though Rilke doesn't name him). Standing in front of Mary in the little room that has suddenly overflowed with his presence, the angel is so enchanted by her ripening beauty that he forgets the message he was sent to announce.

But even in these poems there are hints of the later Rilkean angel. The strongest hint appears in "The Angel," from *New Poems*. Like Jacob's angel, the figure here is the embodiment of challenge, who "with tilted brow dismisses / anything that circumscribes or binds." The poem ends with an image of life-transforming and self-shattering confrontation. If you were to give yourself over to this angel, Rilke tells the reader, some day, some night, the angel's light hands

> *kämen denn . . . dich ringender zu prüfen,*
> *und gingen wie Erzürnte durch das Haus*
> *und griffen dich als ob sie dich erschüfen*
> *und brächen dich aus deiner Form heraus.*

> would come more fiercely to interrogate you,
> and rush to seize you blazing like a star,
> and bend you as if trying to create you,
> and break you open, out of who you are.

But it is in the *Elegies* that the image of the angel becomes truly awe-inspiring. Once you begin to live inside the poem, Rilke's angels seem more and more stunningly authentic. You have the sense that they are not a mere literary symbol, that whatever reality it is that sings its dark music through the classical German dactyls of the verse, it is something that Rilke has penetrated into, not invented.

Rilke had always been a prolific poet. But the completion of his famous novel, *The Notebooks of Malte Laurids Brigge,* in Paris in 1910, had left him shattered and hollow. The book had immersed his imagination in the most difficult realities that he associated with big-city life: loneliness, poverty, alienation, illness, paranoia, despair. His hero's, and his own, sense of ego boundaries grew so paper-thin that, in a weird variation of the Golden Rule, he found himself involuntarily taking on the spiritual devastation of his neighbors, of the whole city. By the time he had finished, he was exhausted. He wandered around Europe for two years, confused, more restless and unhappy than usual, terminally stuck. He wrote a few poems, but they were nothing much. He thought of giving up poetry, of enrolling in medical school. Nothing seemed to make sense.

Then, in the winter of 1912, he received an invitation from a wealthy friend, Princess Marie von Thurn und Taxis-

Hohenlohe, to spend a few months at one of her homes, Duino Castle on the Adriatic Sea. She stayed for a while with a large party of family, guests, and servants then left him there alone.

One morning in late January—the story comes to us from Rilke, through the princess's memoir of him—he received a troublesome business letter, which he had to take care of right away. Outside, a violent north wind blew, though the sun was shining. He climbed down to the bastions, which, jutting out to the east and west, were connected to the foot of the castle by a narrow pathway along cliffs that dropped off two hundred feet into the sea. He walked back and forth, absorbed in the problem of how to answer the letter. Then, all at once, he stopped. From the raging wind, what seemed to him an inhuman voice, the voice of an angel, was calling: *"Who, if I cried out, would hear me among the angels' hierarchies?"* He took out the notebook that he always carried with him and wrote down these words, and a few lines that followed, as if he were taking dictation. Then he climbed back up to his room, set his notebook aside, and (I love this detail) with true Germanic thoroughness, orderly even in the face of cosmic inspiration, first answered the business letter and then continued the poem. By the evening, the whole of "The First Elegy" had been written.

What kind of event was this? That Rilke actually heard the voice of a nonphysical intelligence coming from the storm is possible. That the voice was Rilke's own is certain: it speaks with the poet's "I," in the gorgeous classical rhythms of Rilkean verse. But there is no either/or here. In such intensities of experience, the very idea of outside or inside is irrelevant; psychic resonance spreads through the whole universe of matter; what is given by God is given by the innermost self. Whatever the voice was, angel and self, it came from the depths of life, and it came with an incontrovertible sense of mission. Rilke knew that this poem was to be his own justification.

The angel of the *Duino Elegies* is a figure of total fulfillment, total innerness. In a letter of 1915, Rilke talks about his experience of the Spanish landscape as his own personal analogy to angelic perception:

> There, the external Thing itself—tower, mountain, bridge—already possessed the extraordinary, unsurpassable intensity of those inner equivalents through which one might have wished to represent it. Everywhere appearance and vision merged, as it were, in the object; in each one of them a whole world was revealed, as though an angel who encompassed all space were blind and gazing into himself. This, a world seen no longer from the human point of view, but inside the angel, is perhaps my real task.

"The First Elegy" begins with the voice that Rilke heard in the wind, his own uncried cry of longing and intimation:

> Who, if I cried out, would hear me among the angels'
> hierarchies? and even if one of them pressed me
> suddenly against his heart: I would be consumed
> in that overwhelming existence. For beauty is nothing
> but the beginning of terror, which we still are just able to
> endure,
> and we are so awed because it serenely disdains
> to annihilate us. Every angel is terrifying.

Commenting on this passage in a letter written thirteen years later, Rilke describes the angel in greater detail:

> The "angel" of the Elegies has nothing to do with the angel of the Christian heaven (it has more in common with the angel figures of Islam). The angel of the Elegies is that creature in whom the transformation of the visible into the invisible, which we are accomplishing, already appears in its completion. For the angel of the Elegies, all the

towers and palaces of the past are existent because they have long been invisible, and the still-standing towers and bridges of our reality are already invisible, although still (for us) physically lasting. The angel of the Elegies is that being who guarantees the recognition in the invisible of a higher order of reality.—Therefore "terrifying" for us, because we, its lovers and transformers, still cling to the visible.—All the worlds in the universe are plunging into the invisible as into their next-deeper reality; a few stars intensify immediately and pass away in the infinite consciousness of the angels—, others are entrusted to beings who slowly and laboriously transform them, in whose terrors and delights they attain their next invisible realization. We, let it be emphasized once more, we, in the sense of the Elegies, are these transform-ers of the earth; our whole existence, the flights and plunges of our love, everything, qualifies us for this task (beside which there is, essentially, no other).

The primary description of angels in the *Elegies*—and by far the most beautiful description of them in all litera-ture—appears at the beginning of "The Second Elegy." (The reference is to the apocryphal Book of Tobit, in which the archangel Raphael, appearing in human form, offers him-self as a guide to the young man Tobias on an important journey.)

Every angel is terrifying. And yet, alas,
I invoke you, almost deadly birds of the soul,
knowing about you. Where are the days of Tobias,
when one of you, veiling his radiance, stood at the front
    door,
slightly disguised for the journey, no longer appalling;
(a young man like the one who curiously peeked through
    the window).

But if the archangel now, perilous, from behind the stars
took even one step down toward us: our own heart,
   beating
higher and higher, would beat us to death. Who *are* you?

Early successes, Creation's pampered favorites,
mountain-ranges, peaks growing red in the dawn
of all Beginning,—pollen of the flowering godhead,
joints of pure light, corridors, stairways, thrones,
space formed from essence, shields made of ecstasy,
   storms
of emotion whirled into rapture, and suddenly, alone,
*mirrors:* which scoop up the beauty that has streamed from
   their face
and gather it back, into themselves, entire.

Here the angel becomes pure metaphor, protean, lucid,
breathless. Critics have written long essays about these glori-
ous lines, with their mixture of love and dread and almost
unbearable longing. Ultimately, though, there is not much
one can say. One can only point and admire.

"The Second Elegy" was finished by the end of January
1912, along with the first stanza of the Tenth; the next year
Rilke wrote three-quarters of the Sixth, and then the Third;
and the Fourth in November 1915. But even when the
momentum became sporadic and, after 1915, stopped alto-
gether, with only four Elegies completed, the certainty of his
task remained. It would be a long, excruciating lesson in
patience.

When life occurs at this level of intensity, biography turns
into myth. The myth here resembles that of Psyche and Eros.
The god appears, then is gone; and the abandoned soul must
spend seven years wandering in his traces. Finally, she
arrives. The god enters, she is caught up in a fulfillment
beyond her most extravagant hope. After this, a happy end-
ing seems unnecessary.

Rilke moved from city to city during and after the war,
holding to his certainty and his despair. When at last, at the

Château de Muzot, he found the protected solitude he needed in order to plunge back into himself, he had no suspicion that another masterpiece would arise along with the rest of the Elegies, as their prelude and complement.

On February 2, 1922, he disappeared into the god. It was, he later wrote, "a hurricane in the spirit." For days and nights at a time he stayed in his upstairs room, pacing back and forth, "howling unbelievably vast commands and receiving signals from cosmic space and booming out to them my immense salvos of welcome." By February 5, he had written the twenty-six poems of the first part of *The Sonnets to Orpheus*, "the most mysterious, the most enigmatic dictation I have ever endured and achieved; the whole first part was written down in a single breathless obedience." By February 9, he had finished the *Elegies*. By February 23, he was left with an additional Elegy that replaced the existing Fifth, the brilliant essay on God and sexuality called "The Young Workman's Letter," four shorter poems, and thirty-eight more Sonnets.

This is surely the most astonishing burst of inspiration in the history of literature. Inspiration, because it seems fundamentally different from what other modern poets, even the greatest ones, have known as the process of writing, with all its rawness and groping toward the genuine. There was nothing tentative here. These poems were born perfect; hardly a single word needed to be changed. The whole experience seems to have taken place at an archaic level of consciousness, where the poet is literally the god's or muse's scribe. We are in the presence of something so intensely real that all our rational categories are useless. Who can respond to it without a shudder of awe? Rilke himself did. On February 9, he wrote to his publisher:

> My dear friend,
> late, and though I can barely manage to hold the pen, after several days of huge obedience in the spirit—, you must be told, today, right now, before I try to sleep:

> I have climbed the mountain!
> At last! The Elegies are here, they exist. . . .
>
> So.
> Dear friend, now I can breathe again and, calmly,
> go on to something manageable. For this was larger
> than life—during these days and nights I have
> howled as I did that time in Duino—but, even
> after that struggle there, I didn't know that such a
> storm out of mind and heart could come over a
> person! That one has endured it! that one has
> endured.
>
> Enough. They are here.
> I went out into the cold moonlight and stroked
> the little tower of Muzot as if it were a large ani-
> mal—the ancient walls that granted this to me.

In a sense, completing the *Elegies* meant leaving them behind. The tragic gives place to the rhapsodic; lament modulates into ecstatic appreciation of what can be achieved within our human limitations. "Praise this world to the angel," Rilke says in "The Ninth Elegy,"

> not the unsayable one,
> you can't impress *him* with glorious emotion; in the
>     universe
> where he feels more powerfully, you are a novice. So show
>     him
> something simple which, formed over generations,
> lives as our own, near our hand and within our gaze.

And in *The Sonnets to Orpheus* he sings in utter acceptance of everything that is alive and earthly. Have there ever been poems so radiant with sensuous experience? The taste of an apple, a horse galloping across a meadow, a flower opening at dawn—all are so intensely present in their ephemeral beauty that outer turns into inner, sense into spirit. The wholeness, the transfigured body of these poems, is a return to the simplest human experiences of seeing and breathing, beyond thought: the immense, vibrant, dangerous world that every child lives in. Though it is transcendence, it leaves nothing behind. It is pure precisely because it goes nowhere.

Rilke's angels, those desolating perfections, are not central to the later *Elegies*, and in the *Sonnets* they don't appear at all. They were no longer necessary. Through his long years of patience, he had exorcised them. By the end of the *Sonnets*, Rilke is no longer addressing Orpheus, the primal poet. He has *become* Orpheus and can speak to his personal self from the center of the universe. The cycle is completed. Life resolves in a single breath, and the tree of song that sprang up in the first line of the first Sonnet is transformed into the serene, rooted *I am* that is the *Sonnets'* last word, the word uttered at every moment by each particular form, and also the name of God.

# Duino Elegies

## (1923)

*The property of Princess Marie von Thurn und Taxis-Hohenlohe*
*(1912/1922)*

## DIE ERSTE ELEGIE

Wer, wenn ich schriee, hörte mich denn aus der Engel
Ordnungen? und gesetzt selbst, es nähme
einer mich plötzlich ans Herz: ich verginge von seinem
stärkeren Dasein. Denn das Schöne ist nichts
als des Schrecklichen Anfang, den wir noch grade ertragen,
und wir bewundern es so, weil es gelassen verschmäht,
uns zu zerstören. Ein jeder Engel ist schrecklich.
   Und so verhalt ich mich denn und verschlucke den
      Lockruf
dunkelen Schluchzens. Ach, wen vermögen
wir denn zu brauchen? Engel nicht, Menschen nicht,
und die findigen Tiere merken es schon,
daß wir nicht sehr verläßlich zu Haus sind
in der gedeuteten Welt. Es bleibt uns vielleicht
irgend ein Baum an dem Abhang, daß wir ihn täglich
wiedersähen; es bleibt uns die Straße von gestern
und das verzogene Treusein einer Gewohnheit,
der es bei uns gefiel, und so blieb sie und ging nicht.
   O und die Nacht, die Nacht, wenn der Wind voller
      Weltraum
uns am Angesicht zehrt—, wem bliebe sie nicht, die
      ersehnte,
sanft enttäuschende, welche dem einzelnen Herzen
mühsam bevorsteht. Ist sie den Liebenden leichter?
Ach, sie verdecken sich nur mit einander ihr Los.
   Weißt du's *noch* nicht? Wirf aus den Armen die Leere
zu den Räumen hinzu, die wir atmen; vielleicht daß die
      Vögel
die erweiterte Luft fühlen mit innigerm Flug.

Ja, die Frühlinge brauchten dich wohl. Es muteten manche
Sterne dir zu, daß du sie spürtest. Es hob
sich eine Woge heran im Vergangenen, oder
da du vorüberkamst am geöffneten Fenster,
gab eine Geige sich hin. Das alles war Auftrag.

# THE FIRST ELEGY

Who, if I cried out, would hear me among the angels'
hierarchies? and even if one of them pressed me
suddenly against his heart: I would be consumed
in that overwhelming existence. For beauty is nothing
but the beginning of terror, which we still are just able to
    endure,
and we are so awed because it serenely disdains
to annihilate us. Every angel is terrifying.
    And so I hold myself back and swallow the call-note
of my dark sobbing. Ah, whom can we ever turn to
in our need? Not angels, not humans,
and already the knowing animals are aware
that we are not really at home in
our interpreted world. Perhaps there remains for us
some tree on a hillside, which every day we can take
into our vision; there remains for us yesterday's street
and the loyalty of a habit so much at ease
when it stayed with us that it moved in and never left.
    Oh and night: there is night, when a wind full of infinite
        space
gnaws at our faces. Whom would it not remain for—that
        longed-after,
mildly disillusioning presence, which the solitary heart
so painfully meets. Is it any less difficult for lovers?
But they keep on using each other to hide their own fate.
    Don't you know *yet*? Fling the emptiness out of your arms
into the spaces we breathe; perhaps the birds
will feel the expanded air with more passionate flying.

Yes—the springtimes needed you. Often a star
was waiting for you to notice it. A wave rolled toward you
out of the distant past, or as you walked
under an open window, a violin
yielded itself to your hearing. All this was mission.

Aber bewältigtest du's? Warst du nicht immer
noch von Erwartung zerstreut, als kündigte alles
eine Geliebte dir an? (Wo willst du sie bergen,
da doch die großen fremden Gedanken bei dir
aus und ein gehn und öfters bleiben bei Nacht.)
Sehnt es dich aber, so singe die Liebenden; lange
noch nicht unsterblich genug ist ihr berühmtes Gefühl.
Jene, du neidest sie fast, Verlassenen, die du
so viel liebender fandst als die Gestillten. Beginn
immer von neuem die nie zu erreichende Preisung;
denk: es erhält sich der Held, selbst der Untergang war ihm
nur ein Vorwand, zu sein: seine letzte Geburt.
Aber die Liebenden nimmt die erschöpfte Natur
in sich zurück, als wären nicht zweimal die Kräfte,
dieses zu leisten. Hast du der Gaspara Stampa
denn genügend gedacht, daß irgend ein Mädchen,
dem der Geliebte entging, am gesteigerten Beispiel
dieser Liebenden fühlt: daß ich würde wie sie?
Sollen nicht endlich uns diese ältesten Schmerzen
fruchtbarer werden? Ist es nicht Zeit, daß wir liebend
uns vom Geliebten befrein und es bebend bestehn:
wie der Pfeil die Sehne besteht, um gesammelt im Absprung
*mehr* zu sein als er selbst. Denn Bleiben ist nirgends.

Stimmen, Stimmen. Höre, mein Herz, wie sonst nur
Heilige hörten: daß sie der riesige Ruf
aufhob vom Boden; sie aber knieten,
Unmögliche, weiter und achtetens nicht:
*So* waren sie hörend. Nicht, daß du *Gottes* ertrügest
die Stimme, bei weitem. Aber das Wehende höre,
die ununterbrochene Nachricht, die aus Stille sich bildet.
Es rauscht jetzt von jenen jungen Toten zu dir.
Wo immer du eintratst, redete nicht in Kirchen
zu Rom und Neapel ruhig ihr Schicksal dich an?

But could you accomplish it? Weren't you always
distracted by expectation, as if every event
announced a beloved? (Where can you find a place
to keep her, with all the huge strange thoughts inside you
going and coming and often staying all night.)
But when you feel longing, sing of women in love;
for their famous passion is still not immortal. Sing
of women abandoned and desolate (you envy them, almost)
who could love so much more purely than those who were
    gratified.
Begin again and again the never-attainable praising;
remember: the hero lives on; even his downfall was
merely a pretext for achieving his final birth.
But Nature, spent and exhausted, takes lovers back
into herself, as if there were not enough strength
to create them a second time. Have you imagined
Gaspara Stampa intensely enough so that any girl
deserted by her beloved might be inspired
by that fierce example of soaring, objectless love
and might say to herself, "Perhaps I can be like her"?
Shouldn't this most ancient of sufferings finally grow
more fruitful for us? Isn't it time that we lovingly
freed ourselves from the beloved and, quivering, endured:
as the arrow endures the bowstring's tension, so that
gathered in the snap of release it can be more than
itself. For there is no place where we can remain.

Voices. Voices. Listen, my heart, as only
saints have listened: until the gigantic call lifted them
off the ground; yet they kept on, impossibly,
kneeling and didn't notice at all:
so complete was their listening. Not that you could endure
God's voice—far from it. But listen to the voice of the wind
and the ceaseless message that forms itself out of silence.
It is murmuring toward you now from those who died
    young.
Didn't their fate, whenever you stepped into a church
in Naples or Rome, quietly come to address you?

Oder es trug eine Inschrift sich erhaben dir auf,
wie neulich die Tafel in Santa Maria Formosa.
Was sie mir wollen? leise soll ich des Unrechts
Anschein abtun, der ihrer Geister
reine Bewegung manchmal ein wenig behindert.

Freilich ist es seltsam, die Erde nicht mehr zu bewohnen,
kaum erlernte Gebräuche nicht mehr zu üben,
Rosen, und andern eigens versprechenden Dingen
nicht die Bedeutung menschlicher Zukunft zu geben;
das, was man war in unendlich ängstlichen Händen,
nicht mehr zu sein, und selbst den eigenen Namen
wegzulassen wie ein zerbrochenes Spielzeug.
Seltsam, die Wünsche nicht weiterzuwünschen. Seltsam,
alles, was sich bezog, so lose im Raume
flattern zu sehen. Und das Totsein ist mühsam
und voller Nachholn, daß man allmählich ein wenig
Ewigkeit spürt.—Aber Lebendige machen
alle den Fehler, daß sie zu stark unterscheiden.
Engel (sagt man) wüßten oft nicht, ob sie unter
Lebenden gehn oder Toten. Die ewige Strömung
reißt durch beide Bereiche alle Alter
immer mit sich und übertönt sie in beiden.

Schließlich brauchen sie uns nicht mehr, die Früheent-
      rückten,
man entwöhnt sich des Irdischen sanft, wie man den Brüsten
milde der Mutter entwächst. Aber wir, die so große
Geheimnisse brauchen, denen aus Trauer so oft
seliger Fortschritt entspringt—: *könnten* wir sein ohne sie?
Ist die Sage umsonst, daß einst in der Klage um Linos

Or high up, some eulogy entrusted you with a mission,
as, last year, on the plaque in Santa Maria Formosa.
What they want of me is that I gently remove the appearance
of injustice about their death—which at times
slightly hinders their souls from proceeding onward.

Of course, it is strange to inhabit the earth no longer,
to give up customs one barely had time to learn,
not to see roses and other promising Things
in terms of a human future; no longer to be
what one was in infinitely anxious hands; to leave
even one's own first name behind, forgetting it
as easily as a child abandons a broken toy.
Strange to no longer desire one's desires. Strange
to see meanings that clung together once, floating away
in every direction. And being dead is hard work
and full of retrieval before one can gradually feel
a trace of eternity.—Though the living are wrong to believe
in the too-sharp distinctions which they themselves have
     created.
Angels (they say) don't know whether it is the living
they are moving among, or the dead. The eternal torrent
whirls all ages along in it, through both realms
forever, and their voices are drowned out in its thunderous
     roar.

In the end, those who were carried off early no longer need
     us:
they are weaned from earth's sorrows and joys, as gently as
     children
outgrow the soft breasts of their mothers. But we, who do
     need
such great mysteries, we for whom grief is so often
the source of our spirit's growth—: could we exist without
     *them*?
Is the legend meaningless that tells how, in the lament for
     Linus,

wagende erste Musik dürre Erstarrung durchdrang;
daß erst im erschrockenen Raum, dem ein beinah göttlicher
    Jüngling
plötzlich für immer enttrat, das Leere in jene
Schwingung geriet, die uns jetzt hinreißt und tröstet und
    hilft.

the daring first notes of song pierced through the barren
    numbness;
and then in the startled space which a youth as lovely as a
    god
had suddenly left forever, the Void felt for the first time
that harmony which now enraptures and comforts and helps
    us.

## DIE ZWEITE ELEGIE

Jeder Engel ist schrecklich. Und dennoch, weh mir,
ansing ich euch, fast tödliche Vögel der Seele,
wissend um euch. Wohin sind die Tage Tobiae,
da der Strahlendsten einer stand an der einfachen Haustür,
zur Reise ein wenig verkleidet und schon nicht mehr
    furchtbar;
(Jüngling dem Jüngling, wie er neugierig hinaussah).
Träte der Erzengel jetzt, der gefährliche, hinter den Sternen
eines Schrittes nur nieder und herwärts: hochauf-
schlagend erschlüg uns das eigene Herz. Wer seid ihr?

Frühe Geglückte, ihr Verwöhnten der Schöpfung,
Höhenzüge, morgenrötliche Grate
aller Erschaffung,—Pollen der blühenden Gottheit,
Gelenke des Lichtes, Gänge, Treppen, Throne,
Räume aus Wesen, Schilde aus Wonne, Tumulte
stürmisch entzückten Gefühls und plötzlich, einzeln,
*Spiegel:* die die entströmte eigene Schönheit
wiederschöpfen zurück in das eigene Antlitz.

Denn wir, wo wir fühlen, verflüchtigen; ach wir
atmen uns aus und dahin; von Holzglut zu Holzglut
geben wir schwächern Geruch. Da sagt uns wohl einer:
ja, du gehst mir ins Blut, dieses Zimmer, der Frühling
füllt sich mit dir . . . Was hilfts, er kann uns nicht halten,
wir schwinden in ihm und um ihn. Und jene, die schön sind,
o wer hält sie zurück? Unaufhörlich steht Anschein
auf in ihrem Gesicht und geht fort. Wie Tau von dem
    Frühgras
hebt sich das Unsre von uns, wie die Hitze von einem

# THE SECOND ELEGY

Every angel is terrifying. And yet, alas,
I invoke you, almost deadly birds of the soul,
knowing about you. Where are the days of Tobias,
when one of you, veiling his radiance, stood at the front
    door,
slightly disguised for the journey, no longer appalling;
(a young man like the one who curiously peeked through the
    window).
But if the archangel now, perilous, from behind the stars
took even one step down toward us: our own heart, beating
higher and higher, would beat us to death. Who *are* you?

Early successes, Creation's pampered favorites,
mountain-ranges, peaks growing red in the dawn
of all Beginning,—pollen of the flowering godhead,
joints of pure light, corridors, stairways, thrones,
space formed from essence, shields made of ecstasy, storms
of emotion whirled into rapture, and suddenly, alone,
*mirrors:* which scoop up the beauty that has streamed from
    their face
and gather it back, into themselves, entire.

But we, when moved by deep feeling, evaporate; we
breathe ourselves out and away; from moment to moment
our emotion grows fainter, like a perfume. Though someone
    may tell us:
"Yes, you've entered my bloodstream, the room, the whole
    springtime
is filled with you . . ."—what does it matter? he can't contain
    us,
we vanish inside him and around him. And those who are
    beautiful,
oh who can retain them? Appearance ceaselessly rises
in their face, and is gone. Like dew from the morning grass,
what is ours floats into the air, like steam from a dish

heißen Gericht. O Lächeln, wohin? O Aufschaun:
neue, warme, entgehende Welle des Herzens—;
weh mir: wir *sinds* doch. Schmeckt denn der Weltraum,
in den wir uns lösen, nach uns? Fangen die Engel
wirklich nur Ihriges auf, ihnen Entströmtes,
oder ist manchmal, wie aus Versehen, ein wenig
unseres Wesens dabei? Sind wir in ihre
Züge soviel nur gemischt wie das Vage in die Gesichter
schwangerer Frauen? Sie merken es nicht in dem Wirbel
ihrer Rückkehr zu sich. (Wie sollten sie's merken.)

Liebende könnten, verstünden sie's, in der Nachtluft
wunderlich reden. Denn es scheint, daß uns alles
verheimlicht. Siehe, die Bäume *sind;* die Häuser,
die wir bewohnen, bestehn noch. Wir nur
ziehen allem vorbei wie ein luftiger Austausch.
Und alles ist einig, uns zu verschweigen, halb als
Schande vielleicht und halb als unsägliche Hoffnung.

Liebende, euch, ihr in einander Genügten,
frag ich nach uns. Ihr greift euch. Habt ihr Beweise?
Seht, mir geschiehts, daß meine Hände einander
inne werden oder daß mein gebrauchtes
Gesicht in ihnen sich schont. Das giebt mir ein wenig
Empfindung. Doch wer wagte darum schon zu *sein?*
Ihr aber, die ihr im Entzücken des anderen
zunehmt, bis er euch überwältigt
anfleht: nicht *mehr*—; die ihr unter den Händen
euch reichlicher werdet wie Traubenjahre;
die ihr manchmal vergeht, nur weil der andre
ganz überhand nimmt: euch frag ich nach uns. Ich weiß,
ihr berührt euch so selig, weil die Liebkosung verhält,
weil die Stelle nicht schwindet, die ihr, Zärtliche,
zudeckt; weil ihr darunter das reine
Dauern verspürt. So versprecht ihr euch Ewigkeit fast

of hot food. O smile, where are you going? O upturned
    glance:
new warm receding wave on the sea of the heart . . .
alas, but that is what we *are*. Does the infinite space
we dissolve into, taste of us then? Do the angels really
reabsorb only the radiance that streamed out from
    themselves, or
sometimes, as if by an oversight, is there a trace
of our essence in it as well? Are we mixed in with their
features even as slightly as that vague look
in the faces of pregnant women? They do not notice it
(how could they notice) in their swirling return to
    themselves.

Lovers, if they knew how, might utter strange, marvelous
words in the night air. For it seems that everything
hides us. Look: trees do exist; the houses
that we live in still stand. We alone
fly past all things, as fugitive as the wind.
And all things conspire to keep silent about us, half
out of shame perhaps, half as unutterable hope.

Lovers, gratified in each other, I am asking *you*
about us. You hold each other. Where is your proof?
Look, sometimes I find that my hands have become aware
of each other, or that my time-worn face
shelters itself inside them. That gives me a slight
sensation. But who would dare to exist, just for that?
You, though, who in the other's passion
grow until, overwhelmed, he begs you:
"No *more* . . ."; you who beneath his hands
swell with abundance, like autumn grapes;
you who may disappear because the other has wholly
emerged: I am asking *you* about us. I know,
you touch so blissfully because the caress preserves,
because the place you so tenderly cover
does not vanish; because underneath it
you feel pure duration. So you promise eternity, almost,

von der Umarmung. Und doch, wenn ihr der ersten
Blicke Schrecken besteht und die Sehnsucht am Fenster,
und den ersten gemeinsamen Gang, *ein* Mal durch den
    Garten:
Liebende, *seid* ihrs dann noch? Wenn ihr einer dem andern
euch an den Mund hebt und ansetzt—: Getränk an Getränk:
o wie entgeht dann der Trinkende seltsam der Handlung.

Erstaunte euch nicht auf attischen Stelen die Vorsicht
menschlicher Geste? war nicht Liebe und Abschied
so leicht auf die Schultern gelegt, als wär es aus anderm
Stoffe gemacht als bei uns? Gedenkt euch der Hände,
wie sie drucklos beruhen, obwohl in den Torsen die Kraft
    steht.
Diese Beherrschten wußten damit: so weit sind wirs,
*dieses* ist unser, uns *so* zu berühren; stärker
stemmen die Götter uns an. Doch dies ist Sache der Götter.

Fänden auch wir ein reines, verhaltenes, schmales
Menschliches, einen unseren Streifen Fruchtlands
zwischen Strom und Gestein. Denn das eigene Herz
    übersteigt uns
noch immer wie jene. Und wir können ihm nicht mehr
nachschaun in Bilder, die es besänftigen, noch in
göttliche Körper, in denen es größer sich mäßigt.

from the embrace. And yet, when you have survived
the terror of the first glances, the longing at the window,
and the first walk together, once only, through the garden:
lovers, *are* you the same? When you lift yourselves up
to each other's mouth and your lips join, drink against drink:
oh how strangely each drinker seeps away from his action.

Weren't you astonished by the caution of human gestures
on Attic gravestones? wasn't love and departure
placed so gently on shoulders that it seemed to be made
of a different substance than in our world? Remember the
    hands,
how weightlessly they rest, though there is power in the
    torsos.
These self-mastered figures know: "We can go this far,
this is ours, to touch one another this lightly; the gods
can press down harder upon us. But that is the gods' affair."

If only we too could discover a pure, contained,
human place, our own strip of fruit-bearing soil
between river and rock. For our own heart always exceeds
    us,
as theirs did. And we can no longer follow it, gazing
into images that soothe it or into the godlike bodies
where, measured more greatly, it achieves a greater repose.

## DIE DRITTE ELEGIE

Eines ist, die Geliebte zu singen. Ein anderes, wehe,
jenen verborgenen schuldigen Fluß-Gott des Bluts.
Den sie von weitem erkennt, ihren Jüngling, was weiß er
selbst von dem Herren der Lust, der aus dem Einsamen oft,
ehe das Mädchen noch linderte, oft auch als wäre sie nicht,
ach, von welchem Unkenntlichen triefend, das Gotthaupt
aufhob, aufrufend die Nacht zu unendlichem Aufruhr.
O des Blutes Neptun, o sein furchtbarer Dreizack.
O der dunkele Wind seiner Brust aus gewundener Muschel.
Horch, wie die Nacht sich muldet und höhlt. Ihr Sterne,
stammt nicht von euch des Liebenden Lust zu dem Antlitz
seiner Geliebten? Hat er die innige Einsicht
in ihr reines Gesicht nicht aus dem reinen Gestirn?

Du nicht hast ihm, wehe, nicht seine Mutter
hat ihm die Bogen der Braun so zur Erwartung gespannt.
Nicht an dir, ihn fühlendes Mädchen, an dir nicht
bog seine Lippe sich zum fruchtbarern Ausdruck.
Meinst du wirklich, ihn hätte dein leichter Auftritt
also erschüttert, du, die wandelt wie Frühwind?
Zwar du erschrakst ihm das Herz; doch ältere Schrecken
stürzten in ihn bei dem berührenden Anstoß.
Ruf ihn . . . du rufst ihn nicht ganz aus dunkelem Umgang.
Freilich, er *will*, er entspringt; erleichtert gewöhnt er
sich in dein heimliches Herz und nimmt und beginnt sich.
Aber begann er sich je?
Mutter, *du* machtest ihn klein, du warsts, die ihn anfing;
dir war er neu, du beugtest über die neuen
Augen die freundliche Welt und wehrtest der fremden.

# THE THIRD ELEGY

It is one thing to sing the beloved. Another, alas,
to invoke that hidden, guilty river-god of the blood.
Her young lover, whom she knows from far away—what
    does *he* know of
the lord of desire who often, up from the depths of his
    solitude,
even before she could soothe him, and as though she didn't
    exist,
held up his head, ah, dripping with the unknown,
erect, and summoned the night to an endless uproar.
Oh the Neptune inside our blood, with his appalling trident.
Oh the dark wind from his breast out of that spiraled conch.
Listen to the night as it makes itself hollow. O stars,
isn't it from you that the lover's desire for the face
of his beloved arises? Doesn't his secret insight
into her pure features come from the pure constellations?

Not you, his mother: alas, you were not the one
who bent the arch of his eyebrows into such expectation.
Not for you, girl so aware of him, not for your mouth
did his lips curve themselves into a more fruitful expression.
Do you really think that your gentle steps could have shaken
    him
with such violence, you who move like the morning breeze?
Yes, you did frighten his heart; but more ancient terrors
plunged into him at the shock of that feeling. Call him . . .
but you can't quite call him away from those dark
    companions.
Of course, he *wants* to escape, and he does; relieved, he
    nestles
into your sheltering heart, takes hold, and begins himself.
But did he ever begin himself, really?
Mother, *you* made him small, it was you who started him;
in *your* sight he was new, over his new eyes you arched
the friendly world and warded off the world that was alien.

Wo, ach, hin sind die Jahre, da du ihm einfach
mit der schlanken Gestalt wallendes Chaos vertratst?
Vieles verbargst du ihm so; das nächtlich-verdächtige
     Zimmer
machtest du harmlos, aus deinem Herzen voll Zuflucht
mischtest du menschlichern Raum seinem Nacht-Raum
     hinzu.
Nicht in die Finsternis, nein, in dein näheres Dasein
hast du das Nachtlicht gestellt und es schien wie aus
     Freundschaft.
Nirgends ein Knistern, das du nicht lächelnd erklärtest,
so als wüßtest du längst, *wann* sich die Diele benimmt . . .
Und er horchte und linderte sich. So vieles vermochte
zärtlich dein Aufstehn; hinter den Schrank trat
hoch im Mantel sein Schicksal, und in die Falten des
     Vorhangs
paßte, die leicht sich verschob, seine unruhige Zukunft.

Und er selbst, wie er lag, der Erleichterte, unter
schläfernden Lidern deiner leichten Gestaltung
Süße lösend in den gekosteten Vorschlaf—:
*schien* ein Gehüteter . . . Aber *innen*: wer wehrte,
hinderte innen in ihm die Fluten der Herkunft?
Ach, da *war* keine Vorsicht im Schlafenden; schlafend,
aber träumend, aber in Fiebern: wie er sich ein-ließ.
Er, der Neue, Scheuende, wie er verstrickt war,
mit des innern Geschehns weiterschlagenden Ranken
schon zu Mustern verschlungen, zu würgendem Wachstum,
     zu tierhaft
jagenden Formen. Wie er sich hingab—. Liebte.
Liebte sein Inneres, seines Inneren Wildnis,
diesen Urwald in ihm, auf dessen stummem Gestürztsein
lichtgrün sein Herz stand. Liebte. Verließ es, ging die

Ah, where are the years when you shielded him just by
    placing
your slender form between him and the surging abyss?
How much you hid from him then. The room that filled
    with suspicion
at night: you made it harmless; and out of the refuge of your
    heart
you mixed a more human space in with his night-space.
And you set down the lamp, not in that darkness, but in
your own nearer presence, and it glowed at him like a friend.
There wasn't a creak that your smile could not explain,
as though you had long known just when the floor would do
    that . . .
And he listened and was soothed. So powerful was your
    presence
as you tenderly stood by the bed; his fate,
tall and cloaked, retreated behind the wardrobe, and his
    restless
future, delayed for a while, adapted to the folds of the
    curtain.

And he himself, as he lay there, relieved, with the sweetness
of the gentle world you had made for him dissolving beneath
his drowsy eyelids, into the foretaste of sleep—:
he *seemed* protected . . . But inside: who could ward off,
who could divert, the floods of origin inside him?
Ah, there *was* no trace of caution in that sleeper; sleeping,
yes but dreaming, but flushed with what fevers: how he
    threw himself in.
All at once new, trembling, how he was caught up
and entangled in the spreading tendrils of inner event
already twined into patterns, into strangling undergrowth,
    prowling
bestial shapes. How he submitted—. Loved.
Loved his interior world, his interior wilderness,
that primal forest inside him, where among decayed
    treetrunks
his heart stood, light-green. Loved. Left it, went through

eigenen Wurzeln hinaus in gewaltigen Ursprung,
wo seine kleine Geburt schon überlebt war. Liebend
stieg er hinab in das ältere Blut, in die Schluchten,
wo das Furchtbare lag, noch satt von den Vätern. Und jedes
Schreckliche kannte ihn, blinzelte, war wie verständigt.
Ja, das Entsetzliche lächelte . . . Selten
hast du so zärtlich gelächelt, Mutter. Wie sollte
er es nicht lieben, da es ihm lächelte. *Vor* dir
hat ers geliebt, denn, da du ihn trugst schon,
war es im Wasser gelöst, das den Keimenden leicht macht.

Siehe, wir lieben nicht, wie die Blumen, aus einem
einzigen Jahr; uns steigt, wo wir lieben,
unvordenklicher Saft in die Arme. O Mädchen,
*dies*: daß wir liebten *in* uns, nicht Eines, ein Künftiges,
    sondern
das zahllos Brauende; nicht ein einzelnes Kind,
sondern die Väter, die wie Trümmer Gebirgs
uns im Grunde beruhn; sondern das trockene Flußbett
einstiger Mütter—; sondern die ganze
lautlose Landschaft unter dem wolkigen oder
reinen Verhängnis—: *dies* kam dir, Mädchen, zuvor.

Und du selber, was weißt du—, du locktest
Vorzeit empor in dem Liebenden. Welche Gefühle
wühlten herauf aus entwandelten Wesen. Welche
Frauen haßten dich da. Wasfür finstere Männer
regtest du auf im Geäder des Jünglings? Tote
Kinder wollten zu dir . . . O leise, leise,
tu ein liebes vor ihm, ein verläßliches Tagwerk,—führ ihn
nah an den Garten heran, gieb ihm der Nächte
Übergewicht . . . . . .
                    Verhalt ihn . . . . . .

his own roots and out, into the powerful source
where his little birth had already been outlived. Loving,
he waded down into more ancient blood, to ravines
where Horror lay, still glutted with his fathers. And every
Terror knew him, winked at him like an accomplice.
Yes, Atrocity smiled . . . Seldom
had you smiled so tenderly, mother. How could he help
loving what smiled at him. Even before he knew you,
he had loved it, for already while you carried him inside you,
    it
was dissolved in the water that makes the embryo weightless.

No, we don't accomplish our love in a single year
as the flowers do; an immemorial sap
flows up through our arms when we love. Dear girl,
this: that we loved, inside us, not One who would someday
    appear, but
seething multitudes; not just a single child,
but also the fathers lying in our depths
like fallen mountains; also the dried-up riverbeds
of ancient mothers—; also the whole
soundless landscape under the clouded or clear
sky of its destiny—: all this, my dear, preceded you.

And you yourself, how could you know
what primordial time you stirred in your lover. What
    passions
welled up inside him from departed beings. What
women hated you there. How many dark
sinister men you aroused in his young veins. Dead
children reached out to touch you . . . Oh gently, gently,
let him see you performing, with love, some confident daily
    task,—
lead him out close to the garden, give him what outweighs
the heaviest night . . . . . .
                              Restrain him . . . . . .

## DIE VIERTE ELEGIE

O Bäume Lebens, o wann winterlich?
Wir sind nicht einig. Sind nicht wie die Zug-
vögel verständigt. Überholt und spät,
so drängen wir uns plötzlich Winden auf
und fallen ein auf teilnahmslosen Teich.
Blühn und verdorrn ist uns zugleich bewußt.
Und irgendwo gehn Löwen noch und wissen,
solang sie herrlich sind, von keiner Ohnmacht.

Uns aber, wo wir Eines meinen, ganz,
ist schon des andern Aufwand fühlbar. Feindschaft
ist uns das Nächste. Treten Liebende
nicht immerfort an Ränder, eins im andern,
die sich versprachen Weite, Jagd und Heimat.
    Da wird für eines Augenblickes Zeichnung
ein Grund von Gegenteil bereitet, mühsam,
daß wir sie sähen; denn man ist sehr deutlich
mit uns. Wir kennen den Kontur
des Fühlens nicht: nur, was ihn formt von außen.
    Wer saß nicht bang vor seines Herzens Vorhang?
Der schlug sich auf: die Szenerie war Abschied.
Leicht zu verstehen. Der bekannte Garten,
und schwankte leise: dann erst kam der Tänzer.
Nicht *der*. Genug! Und wenn er auch so leicht tut,
er ist verkleidet und er wird ein Bürger
und geht durch seine Küche in die Wohnung.
    Ich will nicht diese halbgefüllten Masken,
lieber die Puppe. Die ist voll. Ich will
den Balg aushalten und den Draht und ihr
Gesicht aus Aussehn. Hier. Ich bin davor.
Wenn auch die Lampen ausgehn, wenn mir auch
gesagt wird: Nichts mehr—, wenn auch von der Bühne
das Leere herkommt mit dem grauen Luftzug,
wenn auch von meinen stillen Vorfahrn keiner
mehr mit mir dasitzt, keine Frau, sogar

# THE FOURTH ELEGY

O trees of life, when does your winter come?
We are not in harmony, our blood does not forewarn us
like migratory birds'. Late, overtaken,
we force ourselves abruptly onto the wind
and fall to earth at some iced-over lake.
Flowering and fading come to us both at once.
And somewhere lions still roam and never know,
in their majestic power, of any weakness.

But we, while we are intent upon one object,
already feel the pull of another. Conflict
is second nature to us. Aren't lovers
always arriving at each other's boundaries?—
although they promised vastness, hunting, home.

As when for some quick sketch, a wide background
of contrast is laboriously prepared
so that we can see more clearly: we never know
the actual, vital contour of our own
emotions—just what forms them from outside.

Who has not sat, afraid, before his heart's
curtain? It rose: the scenery of farewell.
Easy to recognize. The well-known garden,
which swayed a little. Then the dancer came.
Not *him*. Enough! However lightly he moves,
he's costumed, made up—an ordinary man
who hurries home and walks in through the kitchen.

I won't endure these half-filled human masks;
better, the puppet. It at least is full.
I'll put up with the stuffed skin, the wire, the face
that is nothing but appearance. Here. I'm waiting.
Even if the lights go out; even if someone
tells me "That's all"; even if emptiness
floats toward me in a gray draft from the stage;
even if not one of my silent ancestors
stays seated with me, not one woman, not

der Knabe nicht mehr mit dem braunen Schielaug:
Ich bleibe dennoch. Es giebt immer Zuschaun.

Hab ich nicht recht? Du, der um mich so bitter
das Leben schmeckte, meines kostend, Vater,
den ersten trüben Aufguß meines Müssens,
da ich heranwuchs, immer wieder kostend
und, mit dem Nachgeschmack so fremder Zukunft
beschäftigt, prüftest mein beschlagnes Aufschaun,—
der du, mein Vater, seit du tot bist, oft
in meiner Hoffnung, innen in mir, Angst hast,
und Gleichmut, wie ihn Tote haben, Reiche
von Gleichmut, aufgiebst für mein bißchen Schicksal,
hab ich nicht recht? Und ihr, hab ich nicht recht,
die ihr mich liebtet für den kleinen Anfang
Liebe zu euch, von dem ich immer abkam,
weil mir der Raum in eurem Angesicht,
da ich ihn liebte, überging in Weltraum,
in dem ihr nicht mehr wärt . . . . : wenn mir zumut ist,
zu warten vor der Puppenbühne, nein,
so völlig hinzuschaun, daß, um mein Schauen
am Ende aufzuwiegen, dort als Spieler
ein Engel hinmuß, der die Bälge hochreißt.
Engel und Puppe: dann ist endlich Schauspiel.
Dann kommt zusammen, was wir immerfort
entzwein, indem wir da sind. Dann entsteht
aus unsern Jahreszeiten erst der Umkreis
des ganzen Wandelns. Über uns hinüber
spielt dann der Engel. Sieh, die Sterbenden,
sollten sie nicht vermuten, wie voll Vorwand
das alles ist, was wir hier leisten. Alles
ist nicht es selbst. O Stunden in der Kindheit,
da hinter den Figuren mehr als nur
Vergangnes war und vor uns nicht die Zukunft.
Wir wuchsen freilich und wir drängten manchmal,
bald groß zu werden, denen halb zulieb,

the boy with the immovable brown eye—
I'll sit here anyway. One can always watch.

Am I not right? You, to whom life tasted
so bitter after you took a sip of mine,
the first, gritty infusion of my will,
Father—who, as I grew up, kept on tasting
and, troubled by the aftertaste of so
strange a future, searched my unfocused gaze—
you who, so often since you died, have trembled
for my well-being, within my deepest hope,
relinquishing that calmness which the dead
feel as their very essence, countless realms
of equanimity, for my scrap of life—
tell me, am I not right? And you, dear women
who must have loved me for my small beginning
of love toward you, which I always turned away from
because the space in your features grew, changed,
even while I loved it, into cosmic space,
where you no longer were—: am I not right
to feel as if I *must* stay seated, must
wait before the puppet stage, or, rather,
gaze at it so intensely that at last,
to balance my gaze, an angel has to come and
make the stuffed skins startle into life.
Angel and puppet: a real play, finally.
Then what we separate by our very presence
can come together. And only then, the whole
cycle of transformation will arise,
out of our own life-seasons. Above, beyond us,
the angel plays. If no one else, the dying
must notice how unreal, how full of pretense,
is all that we accomplish here, where nothing
is allowed to be itself. Oh hours of childhood,
when behind each shape more than the past appeared
and what streamed out before us was not the future.
We felt our bodies growing and were at times
impatient to *be* grown up, half for the sake

die andres nicht mehr hatten, als das Großsein.
Und waren doch, in unserem Alleingehn,
mit Dauerndem vergnügt und standen da
im Zwischenraume zwischen Welt und Spielzeug,
an einer Stelle, die seit Anbeginn
gegründet war für einen reinen Vorgang.

Wer zeigt ein Kind, so wie es steht? Wer stellt
es ins Gestirn und giebt das Maß des Abstands
ihm in die Hand? Wer macht den Kindertod
aus grauem Brot, das hart wird,—oder läßt
ihn drin im runden Mund, so wie den Gröps
von einem schönen Apfel? . . . . . . Mörder sind
leicht einzusehen. Aber dies: den Tod,
den ganzen Tod, noch *vor* dem Leben so
sanft zu enthalten und nicht bös zu sein,
ist unbeschreiblich.

of those with nothing left but their grownupness.
Yet were, when playing by ourselves, enchanted
with what alone endures; and we would stand there
in the infinite, blissful space between world and toy,
at a point which, from the earliest beginning,
had been established for a pure event.

Who shows a child as he really is? Who sets him
in his constellation and puts the measuring-rod
of distance in his hand? Who makes his death
out of gray bread, which hardens—or leaves it there
inside his round mouth, jagged as the core
of a sweet apple? . . . . . . Murderers are easy
to understand. But this: that one can contain
death, the whole of death, even before
life has begun, can hold it to one's heart
gently, and not refuse to go on living,
is inexpressible.

## DIE FÜNFTE ELEGIE
*Frau Hertha Koenig zugeeignet*

Wer aber *sind* sie, sag mir, die Fahrenden, diese ein wenig
Flüchtigern noch als wir selbst, die dringend von früh an
wringt ein *wem, wem* zu Liebe
niemals zufriedener Wille? Sondern er wringt sie,
biegt sie, schlingt sie und schwingt sie,
wirft sie und fängt sie zurück; wie aus geölter,
glatterer Luft kommen sie nieder
auf dem verzehrten, von ihrem ewigen
Aufsprung dünneren Teppich, diesem verlorenen
Teppich im Weltall.
Aufgelegt wie ein Pflaster, als hätte der Vorstadt-
Himmel der Erde dort wehe getan.
                             Und kaum dort,
aufrecht, da und gezeigt: des Dastehns
großer Anfangsbuchstab . . . , schon auch, die stärksten
Männer, rollt sie wieder, zum Scherz, der immer
kommende Griff, wie August der Starke bei Tisch
einen zinnenen Teller.

Ach und um diese
Mitte, die Rose des Zuschauns:
blüht und entblättert. Um diesen
Stampfer, den Stempel, den von dem eignen
blühenden Staub getroffnen, zur Scheinfrucht
wieder der Unlust befruchteten, ihrer
niemals bewußten,—glänzend mit dünnster
Oberfläche leicht scheinlächelnden Unlust.

Da: der welke, faltige Stemmer,
der alte, der nur noch trommelt,
eingegangen in seiner gewaltigen Haut, als hätte sie früher
*zwei* Männer enthalten, und einer

# THE FIFTH ELEGY

*Dedicated to Frau Hertha Koenig*

But tell me, who *are* they, these wanderers, even more
transient than we ourselves, who from their earliest days
are savagely wrung out
by a never-satisfied will (for *whose* sake)? Yet it wrings them,
bends them, twists them, swings them and flings them
and catches them again; and falling as if through oiled
slippery air, they land
on the threadbare carpet, worn constantly thinner
by their perpetual leaping, this carpet that is lost
in infinite space.
Stuck on like a bandage, as if the suburban sky
had wounded the earth.
                              And hardly has it appeared
when, standing there, upright, is: the large capital D
that begins Duration . . . , and the always-approaching grip
takes them again, as a joke, even the strongest
men, and crushes them, the way King Augustus the Strong
would crush a pewter plate.

Ah and around this
center: the rose of Onlooking
blooms and unblossoms. Around this
pestle pounding the carpet,
this pistil, fertilized by the pollen
of its own dust, and producing in turn
the specious fruit of displeasure: the unconscious
gaping faces, their thin
surfaces glossy with boredom's specious half-smile.

There: the shriveled-up, wrinkled weight-lifter,
an old man who only drums now,
shrunk in his enormous skin, which looks as if it had once
contained *two* men, and the other

läge nun schon auf dem Kirchhof, und er überlebte den
    andern,
taub und manchmal ein wenig
wirr, in der verwitweten Haut.

Aber der junge, der Mann, als wär er der Sohn eines
    Nackens
und einer Nonne: prall und strammig erfüllt
mit Muskeln und Einfalt.

Oh ihr,
die ein Leid, das noch klein war,
einst als Spielzeug bekam, in einer seiner
langen Genesungen . . . .

Du, der mit dem Aufschlag,
wie nur Früchte ihn kennen, unreif,
täglich hundertmal abfällt vom Baum der gemeinsam
erbauten Bewegung (der, rascher als Wasser, in wenig
Minuten Lenz, Sommer und Herbst hat)—
abfällt und anprallt ans Grab:
manchmal, in halber Pause, will dir ein liebes
Antlitz entstehn hinüber zu deiner selten
zärtlichen Mutter; doch an deinen Körper verliert sich,
der es flächig verbraucht, das schüchtern
kaum versuchte Gesicht . . . Und wieder
klatscht der Mann in die Hand zu dem Ansprung, und eh
    dir
jemals ein Schmerz deutlicher wird in der Nähe des immer
trabenden Herzens, kommt das Brennen der Fußsohln
ihm, seinem Ursprung, zuvor mit ein paar dir
rasch in die Augen gejagten leiblichen Tränen.
Und dennoch, blindlings,
das Lächeln . . . . .

Engel! o nimms, pflücks, das kleinblütige Heilkraut.
Schaff eine Vase, verwahrs! Stells unter jene, uns *noch* nicht
offenen Freuden; in lieblicher Urne

were already lying in the graveyard, while this one lived on
    without him,
deaf and sometimes a little
confused, in the widowed skin.

And the young one over there, the man, who might be the
    son of a neck
and a nun: firm and vigorously filled
with muscles and innocence.

Children,
whom a grief that was still quite small
once received as a toy, during one of its
long convalescences . . . .

You, little boy, who fall down
a hundred times daily, with the thud
that only unripe fruits know, from the tree of mutually
constructed motion (which more quickly than water, in a few
minutes, has its spring, summer, and autumn)—
fall down hard on the grave:
sometimes, during brief pauses, a loving look
toward your seldom affectionate mother tries to be born
in your expression; but it gets lost along the way,
your body consumes it, that timid
scarcely-attempted face . . . And again
the man is clapping his hands for your leap, and before
a pain can become more distinct near your constantly racing
heart, the stinging in your soles rushes ahead of
that other pain, chasing a pair
of physical tears quickly into your eyes.
And nevertheless, blindly,
the smile . . . . .

Oh gather it, Angel, that small-flowered herb of healing.
Create a vase and preserve it. Set it among those joys
not *yet* open to us; on that lovely urn

rühms mit blumiger schwungiger Aufschrift:
                                    'Subrisio Saltat.'

   Du dann, Liebliche,
du, von den reizendsten Freuden
stumm Übersprungne. Vielleicht sind
deine Fransen glücklich für dich—,
oder über den jungen
prallen Brüsten die grüne metallene Seide
fühlt sich unendlich verwöhnt und entbehrt nichts.
Du,
immerfort anders auf alle des Gleichgewichts schwankende
     Waagen
hingelegte Marktfrucht des Gleichmuts,
öffentlich unter den Schultern.

Wo, o *wo* ist der Ort—ich trag ihn im Herzen—,
wo sie noch lange nicht *konnten*, noch von einander
abfieln, wie sich bespringende, nicht recht
paarige Tiere;—
wo die Gewichte noch schwer sind;
wo noch von ihren vergeblich
wirbelnden Stäben die Teller
torkeln . . . . . .

Und plötzlich in diesem mühsamen Nirgends, plötzlich
die unsägliche Stelle, wo sich das reine Zuwenig
unbegreiflich verwandelt—, umspringt
in jenes leere Zuviel.
Wo die vielstellige Rechnung
zahlenlos aufgeht.

Plätze, o Platz in Paris, unendlicher Schauplatz,
wo die Modistin, Madame Lamort,
die ruhlosen Wege der Erde, endlose Bänder,
schlingt und windet und neue aus ihnen
Schleifen erfindet, Rüschen, Blumen, Kokarden, künstliche
     Früchte—, alle
unwahr gefärbt,—für die billigen

praise it with the ornately flowing inscription:
"Subrisio Saltat."

    And you then, my lovely darling,
you whom the most tempting joys
have mutely leapt over. Perhaps
your fringes are happy *for* you—,
or perhaps the green
metallic silk stretched over your firm young breasts
feels itself endlessly indulged and in need of nothing.
You
display-fruit of equanimity,
set out in front of the public, in continual variations
on all the swaying scales of equipoise,
lifted among the shoulders.

Oh *where* is the place—I carry it in my heart—,
where they still were far from mastery, still fell apart
from each other, like mating cattle that someone
has badly paired;—
where the weights are still heavy; where
from their vainly twirling sticks
the plates still wobble
and drop . . . . .

And suddenly in this laborious nowhere, suddenly
the unsayable spot where the pure Too-little is transformed
incomprehensibly—, leaps around and changes
into that empty Too-much;
where the difficult calculation
becomes numberless and resolved.

Squares, oh square in Paris, infinite showplace
where the milliner Madame Lamort
twists and winds the restless paths of the earth,
those endless ribbons, and, from them, designs
new bows, frills, flowers, ruffles, artificial fruits—, all
falsely colored,—for the cheap

Winterhüte des Schicksals.
. . . . . . . . . . . . . . . . . . . .

Engel!: Es wäre ein Platz, den wir nicht wissen, und dorten,
auf unsäglichem Teppich, zeigten die Liebenden, die's hier
bis zum Können nie bringen, ihre kühnen
hohen Figuren des Herzschwungs,
ihre Türme aus Lust, ihre
längst, wo Boden nie war, nur an einander
lehnenden Leitern, bebend,—und könntens,
vor den Zuschauern rings, unzähligen lautlosen Toten:
    Würfen die dann ihre letzten, immer ersparten,
immer verborgenen, die wir nicht kennen, ewig
gültigen Münzen des Glücks vor das endlich
wahrhaft lächelnde Paar auf gestilltem
Teppich?

winter bonnets of Fate.
. . . . . . . . . . . . . . . . . .

Angel!: If there were a place that we didn't know of, and
    there,
on some unsayable carpet, lovers displayed
what they never could bring to mastery here—the bold
exploits of their high-flying hearts,
their towers of pleasure, their ladders
that have long since been standing where there was no
    ground, leaning
just on each other, trembling,—and could *master* all this,
before the surrounding spectators, the innumerable
    soundless dead:
  Would these, then, throw down their final, forever
    saved-up,
forever hidden, unknown to us, eternally valid
coins of happiness before the at last
genuinely smiling pair on the gratified
carpet?

## DIE SECHSTE ELEGIE

Feigenbaum, seit wie lange schon ists mir bedeutend,
wie du die Blüte beinah ganz überschlägst
und hinein in die zeitig entschlossene Frucht,
ungerühmt, drängst dein reines Geheimnis.
Wie der Fontäne Rohr treibt dein gebognes Gezweig
abwärts den Saft und hinan: und er springt aus dem Schlaf,
fast nicht erwachend, ins Glück seiner süßesten Leistung.
Sieh: wie der Gott in den Schwan.

......... Wir aber verweilen,
ach, uns rühmt es zu blühn, und ins verspätete Innre
unserer endlichen Frucht gehn wir verraten hinein.
Wenigen steigt so stark der Andrang des Handelns,
daß sie schon anstehn und glühn in der Fülle des Herzens,
wenn die Verführung zum Blühn wie gelinderte Nachtluft
ihnen die Jugend des Munds, ihnen die Lider berührt:
Helden vielleicht und den frühe Hinüberbestimmten,
denen der gärtnernde Tod anders die Adern verbiegt.
Diese stürzen dahin: dem eigenen Lächeln
sind sie voran, wie das Rossegespann in den milden
muldigen Bildern von Karnak dem siegenden König.

Wunderlich nah ist der Held doch den jugendlich Toten.
    Dauern
ficht ihn nicht an. Sein Aufgang ist Dasein; beständig
nimmt er sich fort und tritt ins veränderte Sternbild
seiner steten Gefahr. Dort fänden ihn wenige. Aber,
das uns finster verschweigt, das plötzlich begeisterte
    Schicksal
singt ihn hinein in den Sturm seiner aufrauschenden Welt.
Hör ich doch keinen wie *ihn*. Auf einmal durchgeht mich
mit der strömenden Luft sein verdunkelter Ton.

Dann, wie verbärg ich mich gern vor der Sehnsucht: O wär
    ich,

# THE SIXTH ELEGY

Fig-tree, for such a long time I have found meaning
in the way you almost completely omit your blossoms
and urge your pure mystery, unproclaimed,
into the early ripening fruit.
Like the curved pipe of a fountain, your arching boughs
     drive the sap
downward and up again: and almost without awakening
it bursts out of sleep, into its sweetest achievement.
Like the god stepping into the swan.
                . . . . . . But *we* still linger, alas,
we, whose pride is in blossoming; we enter the overdue
interior of our final fruit and are already betrayed.
In only a few does the urge to action rise up
so powerfully that they stop, glowing in their heart's
     abundance,
while, like the soft night air, the temptation to blossom
touches their tender mouths, touches their eyelids, softly:
heroes perhaps, and those chosen to disappear early,
whose veins Death the gardener twists into a different
     pattern.
These plunge on ahead: in advance of their own smile
like the team of galloping horses before the triumphant
pharaoh in the mildly hollowed reliefs at Karnak.

The hero is strangely close to those who died young.
     Permanence
does not concern him. He lives in continual ascent,
moving on into the ever-changed constellation
of perpetual danger. Few could find him there. But
Fate, which is silent about us, suddenly grows inspired
and sings him into the storm of his onrushing world.
I hear no one like *him*. All at once I am pierced
by his darkened voice, carried on the streaming air.

Then how gladly I would hide from the longing to be once
     again

wär ich ein Knabe und dürft es noch werden und säße
in die künftigen Arme gestützt und läse von Simson,
wie seine Mutter erst nichts und dann alles gebar.

War er nicht Held schon in dir, o Mutter, begann nicht
dort schon, in dir, seine herrische Auswahl?
Tausende brauten im Schooß und wollten *er* sein,
aber sieh: er ergriff und ließ aus—, wählte und konnte.
Und wenn er Säulen zerstieß, so wars, da er ausbrach
aus der Welt deines Leibs in die engere Welt, wo er weiter
wählte und konnte. O Mütter der Helden, o Ursprung
reißender Ströme! Ihr Schluchten, in die sich
hoch von dem Herzrand, klagend,
schon die Mädchen gestürzt, künftig die Opfer dem Sohn.

Denn hinstürmte der Held durch Aufenthalte der Liebe,
jeder hob ihn hinaus, jeder ihn meinende Herzschlag,
abgewendet schon, stand er am Ende der Lächeln,—anders.

oh a boy once again, with my life before me, to sit
leaning on future arms and reading of Samson,
how from his mother first nothing, then everything, was
    born.

Wasn't he a hero inside you, mother? didn't
his imperious choosing already begin there, in you?
Thousands seethed in your womb, wanting to be *him*,
but look: he grasped and excluded—, chose and prevailed.
And if he demolished pillars, it was when he burst
from the world of your body into the narrower world, where
    again
he chose and prevailed. O mothers of heroes, O sources
of ravaging floods! You ravines into which
virgins have plunged, lamenting,
from the highest rim of the heart, sacrifices to the son.

For whenever the hero stormed through the stations of love,
each heartbeat intended for him lifted him up, beyond it;
and, turning away, he stood there, at the end of all
        smiles,—transfigured.

## DIE SIEBENTE ELEGIE

Werbung nicht mehr, nicht Werbung, entwachsene Stimme,
sei deines Schreies Natur; zwar schrieest du rein wie der
    Vogel,
wenn ihn die Jahreszeit aufhebt, die steigende, beinah
    vergessend,
daß er ein kümmerndes Tier und nicht nur ein einzelnes
    Herz sei,
das sie ins Heitere wirft, in die innigen Himmel. Wie er, so
würbest du wohl, nicht minder—, daß, noch unsichtbar,
dich die Freundin erführ, die stille, in der eine Antwort
langsam erwacht und über dem Hören sich anwärmt,—
deinem erkühnten Gefühl die erglühte Gefühlin.

O und der Frühling begriffe—, da ist keine Stelle,
die nicht trüge den Ton der Verkündigung. Erst jenen
    kleinen
fragenden Auflaut, den, mit steigernder Stille,
weithin umschweigt ein reiner bejahender Tag.
Dann die Stufen hinan, Ruf-Stufen hinan, zum geträumten
Tempel der Zukunft—; dann den Triller, Fontäne,
die zu dem drängenden Strahl schon das Fallen zuvornimmt
im versprechlichen Spiel . . . . Und vor sich, den Sommer.

Nicht nur die Morgen alle des Sommers—, nicht nur
wie sie sich wandeln in Tag und strahlen vor Anfang.
Nicht nur die Tage, die zart sind um Blumen, und oben,
um die gestalteten Bäume, stark und gewaltig.
Nicht nur die Andacht dieser entfalteten Kräfte,
nicht nur die Wege, nicht nur die Wiesen im Abend,
nicht nur, nach spätem Gewitter, das atmende Klarsein,
nicht nur der nahende Schlaf und ein Ahnen, abends . . .

# THE SEVENTH ELEGY

Not wooing, no longer shall wooing, voice that has outgrown
    it,
be the nature of your cry; but instead, you would cry out as
    purely as a bird
when the quickly ascending season lifts him up, nearly
    forgetting
that he is a suffering creature and not just a single heart
being flung into brightness, into the intimate skies. Just like
    him
you would be wooing, not any less purely—, so that, still
unseen, she would sense you, the silent lover in whom a
    reply
slowly awakens and, as she hears you, grows warm,—
the ardent companion to your own most daring emotion.

Oh and springtime would hold it—, everywhere it would
    echo
the song of annunciation. First the small
questioning notes intensified all around
by the sheltering silence of a pure, affirmative day.
Then up the stairs, up the stairway of calls, to the
    dreamed-of
temple of the future—; and then the trill, like a fountain
which, in its rising jet, already anticipates its fall
in a game of promises . . . . And still ahead: summer.

Not only all the dawns of summer—, not only
how they change themselves into day and shine with
    beginning.
Not only the days, so tender around flowers and, above,
around the patterned treetops, so strong, so intense.
Not only the reverence of all these unfolded powers,
not only the pathways, not only the meadows at sunset,
not only, after a late storm, the deep-breathing freshness,
not only approaching sleep, and a premonition . . .

sondern die Nächte! Sondern die hohen, des Sommers,
Nächte, sondern die Sterne, die Sterne der Erde.
O einst tot sein und sie wissen unendlich,
alle die Sterne: denn wie, wie, wie sie vergessen!

Siehe, da rief ich die Liebende. Aber nicht *sie* nur
käme . . . Es kämen aus schwächlichen Gräbern
Mädchen und ständen . . . Denn, wie beschränk ich,
wie, den gerufenen Ruf? Die Versunkenen suchen
immer noch Erde.—Ihr Kinder, ein hiesig
einmal ergriffenes Ding gälte für viele.
Glaubt nicht, Schicksal sei mehr, als das Dichte der
     Kindheit;
wie überholtet ihr oft den Geliebten, atmend,
atmend nach seligem Lauf, auf nichts zu, ins Freie.

Hiersein ist herrlich. Ihr wußtet es, Mädchen, *ihr* auch,
die ihr scheinbar entbehrtet, versankt—, ihr, in den ärgsten
Gassen der Städte, Schwärende, oder dem Abfall
Offene. Denn eine Stunde war jeder, vielleicht nicht
ganz eine Stunde, ein mit den Maßen der Zeit kaum
Meßliches zwischen zwei Weilen—, da sie ein Dasein
hatte. Alles. Die Adern voll Dasein.
Nur, wir vergessen so leicht, was der lachende Nachbar
uns nicht bestätigt oder beneidet. Sichtbar
wollen wirs heben, wo doch das sichtbarste Glück uns
erst zu erkennen sich giebt, wenn wir es innen verwandeln.

Nirgends, Geliebte, wird Welt sein, als innen. Unser
Leben geht hin mit Verwandlung. Und immer geringer
schwindet das Außen. Wo einmal ein dauerndes Haus war,
schlägt sich erdachtes Gebild vor, quer, zu Erdenklichem
völlig gehörig, als ständ es noch ganz im Gehirne.
Weite Speicher der Kraft schafft sich der Zeitgeist, gestaltlos
wie der spannende Drang, den er aus allem gewinnt.

but also the nights! But also the lofty summer
nights, and the stars as well, the stars of the earth.
Oh to be dead at last and know them endlessly,
all the stars: for how, how could we ever forget them!

Look, I was calling for my lover. But not just *she*
would come . . . Out of their fragile graves
girls would arise and gather . . . For how could I limit
the call, once I called it? These unripe spirits keep seeking
the earth.—Children, one earthly Thing
truly experienced, even once, is enough for a lifetime.
Don't think that fate is more than the density of childhood;
how often you outdistanced the man you loved, breathing,
    breathing
after the blissful chase, and passed on into freedom.

*Truly* being here is glorious. Even *you* knew it,
you girls who seemed to be lost, to go under—, in the
    filthiest
streets of the city, festering there, or wide open
for garbage. For each of you had an hour, or perhaps
not even an hour, a barely measurable time
between two moments—, when you were granted a sense
of being. Everything. Your veins flowed with being.
But we can so easily forget what our laughing neighbor
neither confirms nor envies. We want to display it,
to make it visible, though even the most visible happiness
can't reveal itself to us until we transform it, within.

Nowhere, Beloved, will world be but within us. Our life
passes in transformation. And the external
shrinks into less and less. Where once an enduring house
    was,
now a cerebral structure crosses our path, completely
belonging to the realm of concepts, as though it still stood in
    the brain.
Our age has built itself vast reservoirs of power,
formless as the straining energy that it wrests from the earth.

Tempel kennt er nicht mehr. Diese, des Herzens,
      Verschwendung
sparen wir heimlicher ein. Ja, wo noch eins übersteht,
ein einst gebetetes Ding, ein gedientes, geknietes—,
hält es sich, so wie es ist, schon ins Unsichtbare hin.
Viele gewahrens nicht mehr, doch ohne den Vorteil,
daß sie's nun *innerlich* baun, mit Pfeilern und Statuen,
      größer!

Jede dumpfe Umkehr der Welt hat solche Enterbte,
denen das Frühere nicht und noch nicht das Nächste gehört.
Denn auch das Nächste ist weit für die Menschen. *Uns* soll
dies nicht verwirren; es stärke in uns die Bewahrung
der noch erkannten Gestalt.—Dies *stand* einmal unter
      Menschen,
mitten im Schicksal stands, im vernichtenden, mitten
im Nichtwissen-Wohin stand es, wie seiend, und bog
Sterne zu sich aus gesicherten Himmeln. Engel,
*dir* noch zeig ich es, *da!* in deinem Anschaun
steh es gerettet zuletzt, nun endlich aufrecht.
Säulen, Pylone, der Sphinx, das strebende Stemmen,
grau aus vergehender Stadt oder aus fremder, des Doms.

War es nicht Wunder? O staune, Engel, denn *wir* sinds,
wir, o du Großer, erzähls, daß wir solches vermochten, mein
      Atem
reicht für die Rühmung nicht aus. So haben wir dennoch
nicht die Räume versäumt, diese gewährenden, diese
*unseren* Räume. (Was müssen sie fürchterlich groß sein,
da sie Jahrtausende nicht unseres Fühlns überfülln.)
Aber ein Turm war groß, nicht wahr? O Engel, er war es,—
groß, auch noch neben dir? Chartres war groß—, und Musik

Temples are no longer known. It is we who secretly save up
these extravagances of the heart. Where one of them still
    survives,
a Thing that was formerly prayed to, worshipped, knelt
    before—
just as it is, it passes into the invisible world.
Many no longer perceive it, yet miss the chance
to build it *inside* themselves now, with pillars and statues:
    greater.

Each torpid turn of the world has such disinherited ones,
to whom neither the past belongs, nor yet what has nearly
    arrived.
For even the nearest moment is far from mankind. Though
    *we*
should not be confused by this, but strengthened in our task
    of preserving
the still-recognizable form.—This once *stood* among
    mankind,
in the midst of Fate the annihilator, in the midst
of Not-Knowing-Whither, it stood as if enduring, and bent
stars down to it from their safeguarded heavens. Angel,
to *you* I will show it, *there!* in your endless vision
it shall stand, now finally upright, rescued at last.
Pillars, pylons, the Sphinx, the striving thrust
of the cathedral, gray, from a fading or alien city.

Wasn't all this a miracle? Be astonished, Angel, for we
*are* this, O Great One; proclaim that we could achieve this,
    my breath
is too short for such praise. So, after all, we have not
failed to make use of these generous spaces, these
spaces of *ours*. (How frighteningly great they must be,
since thousands of years have not made them overflow with
    our feelings.)
But a tower was great, wasn't it? Oh Angel, it was—
even when placed beside you? Chartres was great—, and
    music

reichte noch weiter hinan und überstieg uns. Doch selbst nur
eine Liebende—, oh, allein am nächtlichen Fenster. . . .
reichte sie dir nicht ans Knie—?
                              Glaub *nicht,* daß ich werbe.
Engel, und würb ich dich auch! Du kommst nicht. Denn
      mein
Anruf ist immer voll Hinweg; wider so starke
Strömung kannst du nicht schreiten. Wie ein gestreckter
Arm ist mein Rufen. Und seine zum Greifen
oben offene Hand bleibt vor dir
offen, wie Abwehr und Warnung,
Unfaßlicher, weitauf.

reached still higher and passed far beyond us. But even
a woman in love—, oh alone at night by her window. . . .
didn't she reach your knee—?

         Don't think that I'm wooing.
Angel, and even if I were, you would not come. For my call
is always filled with departure; against such a powerful
current you cannot move. Like an outstretched arm
is my call. And its hand, held open and reaching up
to seize, remains in front of you, open
as if in defense and warning,
Ungraspable One, far above.

## DIE ACHTE ELEGIE
*Rudolf Kassner zugeeignet*

Mit allen Augen sieht die Kreatur
das Offene. Nur unsre Augen sind
wie umgekehrt und ganz um sie gestellt
als Fallen, rings um ihren freien Ausgang.
Was draußen *ist,* wir wissens aus des Tiers
Antlitz allein; denn schon das frühe Kind
wenden wir um und zwingens, daß es rückwärts
Gestaltung sehe, nicht das Offne, das
im Tiergesicht so tief ist. Frei von Tod.
*Ihn* sehen wir allein; das freie Tier
hat seinen Untergang stets hinter sich
und vor sich Gott, und wenn es geht, so gehts
in Ewigkeit, so wie die Brunnen gehen.
    *Wir* haben nie, nicht einen einzigen Tag,
den reinen Raum vor uns, in den die Blumen
unendlich aufgehn. Immer ist es Welt
und niemals Nirgends ohne Nicht: das Reine,
Unüberwachte, das man atmet und
unendlich *weiß* und nicht begehrt. Als Kind
verliert sich eins im Stilln an dies und wird
gerüttelt. Oder jener stirbt und ists.
Denn nah am Tod sieht man den Tod nicht mehr
und starrt *hinaus,* vielleicht mit großem Tierblick.
Liebende, wäre nicht der andre, der
die Sicht verstellt, sind nah daran und staunen . . .
Wie aus Versehn ist ihnen aufgetan
hinter dem andern . . . Aber über ihn
kommt keiner fort, und wieder wird ihm Welt.
Der Schöpfung immer zugewendet, sehn
wir nur auf ihr die Spiegelung des Frein,
von uns verdunkelt. Oder daß ein Tier,
ein stummes, aufschaut, ruhig durch uns durch.

# THE EIGHTH ELEGY

*Dedicated to Rudolf Kassner*

With all its eyes the natural world looks out
into the Open. Only *our* eyes are turned
backward, and surround plant, animal, child
like traps, as they emerge into their freedom.
We know what is really out there only from
the animal's gaze; for we take the very young
child and force it around, so that it sees
objects—not the Open, which is so .
deep in animals' faces. Free from death.
We, only, can see death; the free animal
has its decline in back of it, forever,
and God in front, and when it moves, it moves
already in eternity, like a fountain.
    Never, not for a single day, do *we* have
before us that pure space into which flowers
endlessly open. Always there is World
and never Nowhere without the No: that pure
unseparated element which one breathes
without desire and endlessly *knows*. A child
may wander there for hours, through the timeless
stillness, may get lost in it and be
shaken back. Or someone dies and *is* it.
For, nearing death, one doesn't see death; but stares
beyond, perhaps with an animal's vast gaze.
Lovers, if the beloved were not there
blocking the view, are close to it, and marvel . . .
As if by some mistake, it opens for them
behind each other . . . But neither can move past
the other, and it changes back to World.
Forever turned toward objects, we see in them
the mere reflection of the realm of freedom,
which we have dimmed. Or when some animal
mutely, serenely, looks us through and through.

Dieses heißt Schicksal: gegenüber sein
und nichts als das und immer gegenüber.

Wäre Bewußtheit unsrer Art in dem
sicheren Tier, das uns entgegenzieht
in anderer Richtung—, riß es uns herum
mit seinem Wandel. Doch sein Sein ist ihm
unendlich, ungefaßt und ohne Blick
auf seinen Zustand, rein, so wie sein Ausblick.
Und wo wir Zukunft sehn, dort sieht es Alles
und sich in Allem und geheilt für immer.

Und doch ist in dem wachsam warmen Tier
Gewicht und Sorge einer großen Schwermut.
Denn ihm auch haftet immer an, was uns
oft überwältigt,—die Erinnerung,
als sei schon einmal das, wonach man drängt,
näher gewesen, treuer und sein Anschluß
unendlich zärtlich. Hier ist alles Abstand,
und dort wars Atem. Nach der ersten Heimat
ist ihm die zweite zwitterig und windig.
      O Seligkeit der *kleinen* Kreatur,
die immer *bleibt* im Schooße, der sie austrug;
o Glück der Mücke, die noch *innen* hüpft,
selbst wenn sie Hochzeit hat: denn Schooß ist Alles.
Und sieh die halbe Sicherheit des Vogels,
der beinah beides weiß aus seinem Ursprung,
als wär er eine Seele der Etrusker,
aus einem Toten, den ein Raum empfing,
doch mit der ruhenden Figur als Deckel.
Und wie bestürzt ist eins, das fliegen muß
und stammt aus einem Schooß. Wie vor sich selbst
erschreckt, durchzuckts die Luft, wie wenn ein Sprung
durch eine Tasse geht. So reißt die Spur
der Fledermaus durchs Porzellan des Abends.

Und wir: Zuschauer, immer, überall,
dem allen zugewandt und nie hinaus!

That is what fate means: to be opposite,
to be opposite and nothing else, forever.

If the animal moving toward us so securely
in a different direction had our kind of
consciousness—, it would wrench us around and drag us
along its path. But it feels its life as boundless,
unfathomable, and without regard
to its own condition: pure, like its outward gaze.
And where we see the future, it sees all time
and itself within all time, forever healed.

Yet in the alert, warm animal there lies
the pain and burden of an enormous sadness.
For it too feels the presence of what often
overwhelms us: a memory, as if
the element we keep pressing toward was once
more intimate, more true, and our communion
infinitely tender. Here all is distance;
there it was breath. After that first home,
the second seems ambiguous and drafty.
　　Oh bliss of the *tiny* creature which remains
forever inside the womb that was its shelter;
joy of the gnat which, still *within,* leaps up
even at its marriage: for everything is womb.
And look at the half-assurance of the bird,
which knows both inner and outer, from its source,
as if it were the soul of an Etruscan,
flown out of a dead man received inside a space,
but with his reclining image as the lid.
And how bewildered is any womb-born creature
that has to fly. As if terrified and fleeing
from itself, it zigzags through the air, the way
a crack runs through a teacup. So the bat
quivers across the porcelain of evening.

And we: spectators, always, everywhere,
turned toward the world of objects, never outward.

Uns überfüllts. Wir ordnens. Es zerfällt.
Wir ordnens wieder und zerfallen selbst.

Wer hat uns also umgedreht, daß wir,
was wir auch tun, in jener Haltung sind
von einem, welcher fortgeht? Wie er auf
dem letzten Hügel, der ihm ganz sein Tal
noch einmal zeigt, sich wendet, anhält, weilt—,
so leben wir und nehmen immer Abschied.

It fills us. We arrange it. It breaks down.
We rearrange it, then break down ourselves.

Who has twisted us around like this, so that
no matter what we do, we are in the posture
of someone going away? Just as, upon
the farthest hill, which shows him his whole valley
one last time, he turns, stops, lingers—,
so we live here, forever taking leave.

## DIE NEUNTE ELEGIE

Warum, wenn es angeht, also die Frist des Daseins
hinzubringen, als Lorbeer, ein wenig dunkler als alle
andere Grün, mit kleinen Wellen an jedem
Blattrand (wie eines Windes Lächeln)—: warum dann
Menschliches müssen—und, Schicksal vermeidend,
sich sehnen nach Schicksal? . . .

                         Oh, *nicht*, weil Glück *ist*,
dieser voreilige Vorteil eines nahen Verlusts.
Nicht aus Neugier, oder zur Übung des Herzens,
das auch im Lorbeer *wäre* . . . . .

Aber weil Hiersein viel ist, und weil uns scheinbar
alles das Hiesige braucht, dieses Schwindende, das
seltsam uns angeht. Uns, die Schwindendsten. *Ein* Mal
jedes, nur *ein* Mal. *Ein* Mal und nichtmehr. Und wir auch
*ein* Mal. Nie wieder. Aber dieses
*ein* Mal gewesen zu sein, wenn auch nur *ein* Mal:
*irdisch* gewesen zu sein, scheint nicht widerrufbar.

Und so drängen wir uns und wollen es leisten,
wollens enthalten in unsern einfachen Händen,
im überfüllteren Blick und im sprachlosen Herzen.
Wollen es werden.—Wem es geben? Am liebsten
alles behalten für immer . . . Ach, in den andern Bezug,
wehe, was nimmt man hinüber? Nicht das Anschaun, das
    hier
langsam erlernte, und kein hier Ereignetes. Keins.
Also die Schmerzen. Also vor allem das Schwersein,
also der Liebe lange Erfahrung,—also
lauter Unsägliches. Aber später,
unter den Sternen, was solls: *die* sind *besser* unsäglich.
Bringt doch der Wanderer auch vom Hange des Bergrands

# THE NINTH ELEGY

Why, if this interval of being can be spent serenely
in the form of a laurel, slightly darker than all
other green, with tiny waves on the edges
of every leaf (like the smile of a breeze)—: why then
have to be human—and, escaping from fate,
keep longing for fate? . . .

                     Oh *not* because happiness *exists*,
that too-hasty profit snatched from approaching loss.
Not out of curiosity, not as practice for the heart, which
would exist in the laurel too . . . . .

But because *truly* being here is so much; because everything
   here
apparently needs us, this fleeting world, which in some
   strange way
keeps calling to us. Us, the most fleeting of all.
*Once* for each thing. Just once; no more. And we too,
just once. And never again. But to have been
this once, completely, even if only once:
to have been at one with the earth, seems beyond undoing.

And so we keep pressing on, trying to achieve it,
trying to hold it firmly in our simple hands,
in our overcrowded gaze, in our speechless heart.
Trying to become it.—Whom can we give it to? We would
hold on to it all, forever . . . Ah, but what can we take along
into that other realm? Not the art of looking,
which is learned so slowly, and nothing that happened here.
   Nothing.
The sufferings, then. And, above all, the heaviness,
and the long experience of love,—just what is wholly
unsayable. But later, among the stars,
what good is it—*they* are *better* as they are: unsayable.
For when the traveler returns from the mountain-slopes into
   the valley,

nicht eine Hand voll Erde ins Tal, die Allen unsägliche,
    sondern
ein erworbenes Wort, reines, den gelben und blaun
Enzian. Sind wir vielleicht *hier,* um zu sagen: Haus,
Brücke, Brunnen, Tor, Krug, Obstbaum, Fenster,—
höchstens: Säule, Turm. . . . aber zu *sagen,* verstehs,
oh zu sagen *so,* wie selber die Dinge niemals
innig meinten zu sein. Ist nicht die heimliche List
dieser verschwiegenen Erde, wenn sie die Liebenden drängt,
daß sich in ihrem Gefühl jedes und jedes entzückt?
Schwelle: was ists für zwei
Liebende, daß sie die eigne ältere Schwelle der Tür
ein wenig verbrauchen, auch sie, nach den vielen vorher
und vor den Künftigen . . . . . , leicht.

*Hier* ist des *Säglichen* Zeit, *hier* seine Heimat.
Sprich und bekenn. Mehr als je
fallen die Dinge dahin, die erlebbaren, denn,
was sie verdrängend ersetzt, ist ein Tun ohne Bild.
Tun unter Krusten, die willig zerspringen, sobald
innen das Handeln entwächst und sich anders begrenzt.
Zwischen den Hämmern besteht
unser Herz, wie die Zunge
zwischen den Zähnen, die doch,
dennoch, die preisende bleibt.

Preise dem Engel die Welt, nicht die unsägliche, *ihm*
kannst du nicht großtun mit herrlich Erfühltem; im Weltall,
wo er fühlender fühlt, bist du ein Neuling. Drum zeig
ihm das Einfache, das, von Geschlecht zu Geschlechtern
    gestaltet,
als ein Unsriges lebt, neben der Hand und im Blick.
Sag ihm die Dinge. Er wird staunender stehn; wie du
    standest
bei dem Seiler in Rom, oder beim Töpfer am Nil.

he brings, not a handful of earth, unsayable to others, but
    instead
some word he has gained, some pure word, the yellow and
    blue
gentian. Perhaps we are *here* in order to say: house,
bridge, fountain, gate, pitcher, fruit-tree, window—
at most: column, tower. . . . But to *say* them, you must
    understand,
oh to say them *more* intensely than the Things themselves
ever dreamed of existing. Isn't the secret intent
of this taciturn earth, when it forces lovers together,
that inside their boundless emotion all things may shudder
    with joy?
Threshold: what it means for two lovers
to be wearing down, imperceptibly, the ancient threshold of
    their door—
they too, after the many who came before them
and before those to come . . . . , lightly.

*Here* is the time for the *sayable, here* is its homeland.
Speak and bear witness. More than ever
the Things that we might experience are vanishing, for
what crowds them out and replaces them is an imageless act.
An act under a shell, which easily cracks open as soon as
the business inside outgrows it and seeks new limits.
Between the hammers our heart
endures, just as the tongue does
between the teeth and, despite that,
still is able to praise.

Praise this world to the angel, not the unsayable one,
you can't impress *him* with glorious emotion; in the universe
where he feels more powerfully, you are a novice. So show
    him
something simple which, formed over generations,
lives as our own, near our hand and within our gaze.
Tell him of Things. He will stand astonished; as *you* stood
by the rope-maker in Rome or the potter along the Nile.

Zeig ihm, wie glücklich ein Ding sein kann, wie schuldlos
    und unser,
wie selbst das klagende Leid rein zur Gestalt sich
    entschließt,
dient als ein Ding, oder stirbt in ein Ding—, und jenseits
selig der Geige entgeht.—Und diese, von Hingang
lebenden Dinge verstehn, daß du sie rühmst; vergänglich,
traun sie ein Rettendes uns, den Vergänglichsten, zu.
Wollen, wir sollen sie ganz im unsichtbarn Herzen
    verwandeln
in—o unendlich—in uns! Wer wir am Ende auch seien.

Erde, ist es nicht dies, was du willst: *unsichtbar*
in uns erstehn?—Ist es dein Traum nicht,
einmal unsichtbar zu sein?—Erde! unsichtbar!
Was, wenn Verwandlung nicht, ist dein drängender
    Auftrag?
Erde, du liebe, ich will. Oh glaub, es bedürfte
nicht deiner Frühlinge mehr, mich dir zu gewinnen—, *einer,*
ach, ein einziger ist schon dem Blute zu viel.
Namenlos bin ich zu dir entschlossen, von weit her.
Immer warst du im Recht, und dein heiliger Einfall
ist der vertrauliche Tod.

Siehe, ich lebe. Woraus? Weder Kindheit noch Zukunft
werden weniger . . . . . Überzähliges Dasein
entspringt mir im Herzen.

Show him how happy a Thing can be, how innocent and
    ours,
how even lamenting grief purely decides to take form,
serves as a Thing, or dies into a Thing—, and blissfully
escapes far beyond the violin.—And these Things,
which live by perishing, know you are praising them;
    transient,
they look to us for deliverance: us, the most transient of all.
They want us to change them, utterly, in our invisible heart,
within—oh endlessly—within us! Whoever we may be at
    last.

Earth, isn't this what you want: to arise within us,
*invisible*? Isn't it your dream
to be wholly invisible someday?—O Earth: invisible!
What, if not transformation, is your urgent command?
Earth, my dearest, I will. Oh believe me, you no longer
need your springtimes to win me over—one of them,
ah, even one, is already too much for my blood.
Unspeakably I have belonged to you, from the first.
You were always right, and your holiest inspiration
is our intimate companion, Death.

Look, I am living. On what? Neither childhood nor future
grows any smaller . . . . . Superabundant being
wells up in my heart.

## DIE ZEHNTE ELEGIE

Daß ich dereinst, an dem Ausgang der grimmigen Einsicht,
Jubel und Ruhm aufsinge zustimmenden Engeln.
Daß von den klar geschlagenen Hämmern des Herzens
keiner versage an weichen, zweifelnden oder
reißenden Saiten. Daß mich mein strömendes Antlitz
glänzender mache; daß das unscheinbare Weinen
blühe. O wie werdet ihr dann, Nächte, mir lieb sein,
gehärmte. Daß ich euch knieender nicht, untröstliche
    Schwestern,
hinnahm, nicht in euer gelöstes
Haar mich gelöster ergab. Wir, Vergeuder der Schmerzen.
Wie wir sie absehn voraus, in die traurige Dauer,
ob sie nicht enden vielleicht. Sie aber sind ja
unser winterwähriges Laub, unser dunkeles Sinngrün,
*eine* der Zeiten des heimlichen Jahres—, nicht nur
Zeit—, sind Stelle, Siedelung, Lager, Boden, Wohnort.

Freilich, wehe, wie fremd sind die Gassen der Leid-Stadt,
wo in der falschen, aus Übertönung gemachten
Stille, stark, aus der Gußform des Leeren der Ausguß
prahlt: der vergoldete Lärm, das platzende Denkmal.
O, wie spurlos zerträte ein Engel ihnen den Trostmarkt,
den die Kirche begrenzt, ihre fertig gekaufte:
reinlich und zu und enttäuscht wie ein Postamt am Sonntag.
Draußen aber kräuseln sich immer die Ränder von
    Jahrmarkt.
Schaukeln der Freiheit! Taucher und Gaukler des Eifers!
Und des behübschten Glücks figürliche Schießstatt,
wo es zappelt von Ziel und sich blechern benimmt,
wenn ein Geschickterer trifft. Von Beifall zu Zufall
taumelt er weiter; denn Buden jeglicher Neugier
werben, trommeln und plärrn. Für Erwachsene aber
ist noch besonders zu sehn, wie das Geld sich vermehrt,
    anatomisch,

## THE TENTH ELEGY

Someday, emerging at last from the violent insight,
let me sing out jubilation and praise to assenting angels.
Let not even one of the clearly-struck hammers of my heart
fail to sound because of a slack, a doubtful,
or a broken string. Let my joyfully streaming face
make me more radiant; let my hidden weeping arise
and blossom. How dear you will be to me then, you nights
of anguish. Why didn't I kneel more deeply to accept you,
inconsolable sisters, and, surrendering, lose myself
in your loosened hair. How we squander our hours of pain.
How we gaze beyond them into the bitter duration
to see if they have an end. Though they are really
our winter-enduring foliage, our dark evergreen,
*one* season in our inner year—, not only a season
in time—, but are place and settlement, foundation and soil
    and home.

But how alien, alas, are the streets of the city of grief,
where, in the false silence formed of continual uproar,
the figure cast from the mold of emptiness stoutly
swaggers: the gilded noise, the bursting memorial.
Oh how completely an angel would stamp out their market
    of solace,
bounded by the church with its ready-made consolations:
clean and disenchanted and shut as a post-office on Sunday.
Farther out, though, the city's edges are curling with
    carnival.
Swings of freedom! Divers and jugglers of zeal!
And the shooting-gallery's targets of prettified happiness,
which jump and kick back with a tinny sound
when hit by some better marksman. From cheers to chance
he goes staggering on, as booths with all sorts of attractions
are wooing, drumming, and bawling. For adults only
there is something special to see: how money multiplies,
    naked,

nicht zur Belustigung nur: der Geschlechtsteil des Gelds,
alles, das Ganze, der Vorgang—, das unterrichtet und macht
fruchtbar . . . . . . . .
. . . . Oh aber gleich darüber hinaus,
hinter der letzten Planke, beklebt mit Plakaten des 'Todlos',
jenes bitteren Biers, das den Trinkenden süß scheint,
wenn sie immer dazu frische Zerstreuungen kaun . . . ,
gleich im Rücken der Planke, gleich dahinter, ists *wirklich.*
Kinder spielen, und Liebende halten einander,—abseits,
ernst, im ärmlichen Gras, und Hunde haben Natur.
Weiter noch zieht es den Jüngling; vielleicht, daß er eine
        junge
Klage liebt . . . . . Hinter ihr her kommt er in Wiesen. Sie
        sagt:
—Weit. Wir wohnen dort draußen . . . .
                                Wo? Und der Jüngling
folgt. Ihn rührt ihre Haltung. Die Schulter, der Hals—,
        vielleicht
ist sie von herrlicher Herkunft. Aber er läßt sie, kehrt um,
wendet sich, winkt . . . Was solls? Sie ist eine Klage.

Nur die jungen Toten, im ersten Zustand
zeitlosen Gleichmuts, dem der Entwöhnung,
folgen ihr liebend. Mädchen
wartet sie ab und befreundet sie. Zeigt ihnen leise,
was sie an sich hat. Perlen des Leids und die feinen
Schleier der Duldung.—Mit Jünglingen geht sie
schweigend.

Aber dort, wo sie wohnen, im Tal, der Älteren eine, der
        Klagen,
nimmt sich des Jünglinges an, wenn er fragt:—Wir waren,
sagt sie, ein Großes Geschlecht, einmal, wir Klagen. Die
        Väter

right there on stage, money's genitals, nothing concealed,
the whole action—, educational, and guaranteed
to increase your potency . . . . . . . . .
. . . . Oh, but a little farther,
beyond the last of the billboards, plastered with signs for
    "Deathless,"
that bitter beer which seems so sweet to its drinkers
as long as they chew fresh distractions in between sips . . . ,
just in back of the billboard, just behind, the view becomes
    *real.*
Children are playing, and lovers are holding hands, to the
    side,
solemnly in the meager grass, and dogs are doing what is
    natural.
The young man is drawn on, farther; perhaps he is in love
    with a young
Lament . . . . . He comes out behind her, into the meadows.
    She says:
—It's a long walk. We live way out there . . . .
                                Where? And the youth
follows. He is touched by her manner. Her shoulders, her
    neck—, perhaps
she is of noble descent. But he leaves her, turns around,
looks back, waves . . . What's the use? She is a Lament.

Only those who died young, in their first condition
of timeless equanimity, while they are being weaned,
follow her lovingly. She waits
for girls and befriends them. Shows them, gently,
what she is wearing. Pearls of grief and the fine-spun
veils of patience.—With young men she walks
in silence.

But there, in the valley, where they live, one of the elder
    Laments
answers the youth when he questions her:—Long ago,
she says, we Laments were a powerful race. Our forefathers
    worked

trieben den Bergbau dort in dem großen Gebirg; bei
　　Menschen
findest du manchmal ein Stück geschliffenes Ur-Leid
oder, aus altem Vulkan, schlackig versteinerten Zorn.
Ja, das stammte von dort. Einst waren wir reich.—

Und sie leitet ihn leicht durch die weite Landschaft der
　　Klagen,
zeigt ihm die Säulen der Tempel oder die Trümmer
jener Burgen, von wo Klage-Fürsten das Land
einstens weise beherrscht. Zeigt ihm die hohen
Tränenbäume und Felder blühender Wehmut,
(Lebendige kennen sie nur als sanftes Blattwerk);
zeigt ihm die Tiere der Trauer, weidend,—und manchmal
schreckt ein Vogel und zieht, flach ihnen fliegend durchs
　　Aufschaun,
weithin das schriftliche Bild seines vereinsamten Schreis.—
Abends führt sie ihn hin zu den Gräbern der Alten
aus dem Klage-Geschlecht, den Sibyllen und Warn-Herrn.
Naht aber Nacht, so wandeln sie leiser, und bald
mondet empor, das über Alles
wachende Grab-Mal. Brüderlich jenem am Nil,
der erhabene Sphinx—: der verschwiegenen Kammer
Antlitz.
Und sie staunen dem krönlichen Haupt, das für immer,
schweigend, der Menschen Gesicht
auf die Waage der Sterne gelegt.

Nicht erfaßt es sein Blick, im Frühtod
schwindelnd. Aber ihr Schaun,
hinter dem Pschent-Rand hervor, scheucht es die Eule. Und
　　sie,
streifend im langsamen Abstrich die Wange entlang,
jene der reifesten Rundung,
zeichnet weich in das neue
Totengehör, über ein doppelt
aufgeschlagenes Blatt, den unbeschreiblichen Umriß.

*

the mines, up there in the mountain-range; sometimes even
among men you can find a polished nugget of primal grief
or a chunk of petrified rage from the slag of an ancient
    volcano.
Yes, that came from up there. We used to be rich.—

And gently she guides him through the vast landscape of
    Lament,
shows him the pillars of the temples, and the ruined walls
of those castles from which, long ago, the princes of Lament
wisely ruled the land. Shows him the tall
trees of tears and the fields of blossoming grief
(the living know it just as a mild green shrub);
shows him the herds of sorrow, grazing,—and sometimes
a startled bird, flying low through their upward gaze,
far away traces the image of its solitary cry.—
In the twilight she leads him out to the graves of the elders
who gave warning to the race of Laments, the sibyls and
    prophets.
But as night approaches, they move more softly, and soon
the sepulchre rises up
like a moon, watching over everything. Brother to the one on
    the Nile,
the lofty Sphinx—: the taciturn chamber's
countenance.
And they look in wonder at the regal head that has silently
lifted the human face
to the scale of the stars, forever.

Still dizzy from recent death, his sight
cannot grasp it. But her gaze
frightens an owl from behind the rim of the crown. And the
    bird,
with slow downstrokes, brushes along the cheek,
the one with the fuller curve,
and faintly, in the dead youth's new
sense of hearing, as upon a double
unfolded page, it sketches the indescribable outline.

*

Und höher, die Sterne. Neue. Die Sterne des Leidlands.
Langsam nennt sie die Klage:—Hier,
siehe: den *Reiter*, den *Stab*, und das vollere Sternbild
nennen sie: *Fruchtkranz*. Dann, weiter, dem Pol zu:
*Wiege; Weg; Das Brennende Buch; Puppe; Fenster*.
Aber im südlichen Himmel, rein wie im Innern
einer gesegneten Hand, das klar erglänzende *M*,
das die Mütter bedeutet . . . . . . —

Doch der Tote muß fort, und schweigend bringt ihn die
     ältere
Klage bis an die Talschlucht,
wo es schimmert im Mondschein:
die Quelle der Freude. In Ehrfurcht
nennt sie sie, sagt:—Bei den Menschen
ist sie ein tragender Strom.—

Stehn am Fuß des Gebirgs.
Und da umarmt sie ihn, weinend.

Einsam steigt er dahin, in die Berge des Ur-Leids.
Und nicht einmal sein Schritt klingt aus dem tonlosen Los.

*

Aber erweckten sie uns, die unendlich Toten, ein Gleichnis,
siehe, sie zeigten vielleicht auf die Kätzchen der leeren
Hasel, die hängenden, oder
meinten den Regen, der fällt auf dunkles Erdreich im
     Frühjahr.—

Und wir, die an *steigendes* Glück
denken, empfänden die Rührung,
die uns beinah bestürzt,
wenn ein Glückliches *fällt*.

And higher, the stars. The new stars of the land of grief.
Slowly the Lament names them:—Look, there:
the *Rider,* the *Staff,* and the larger constellation
called *Garland of Fruit.* Then, farther up toward the Pole:
*Cradle; Path; The Burning Book; Puppet; Window.*
But there, in the southern sky, pure as the lines
on the palm of a blessed hand, the clear sparkling *M*
that stands for Mothers . . . . . . —

But the dead youth must go on by himself, and silently the
  elder Lament
takes him as far as the ravine,
where shimmering in the moonlight
is the fountainhead of joy. With reverence
she names it and says: —Among men
it is a mighty stream.—

They stand at the foot of the mountain-range.
And she embraces him, weeping.

Alone, he climbs on, up the mountains of primal grief.
And not once do his footsteps echo from the soundless path.

*

But if the endlessly dead awakened a symbol in us,
perhaps they would point to the catkins hanging from the
  bare
branches of the hazel-trees, or
would evoke the raindrops that fall onto the dark earth in
  springtime.—

And we, who have always thought
of happiness as *rising,* would feel
the emotion that almost overwhelms us
whenever a happy thing *falls.*

# *Appendix to Duino Elegies*

## [FRAGMENT EINER ELEGIE]

Soll ich die Städte rühmen, die überlebenden
(die ich anstaunte) großen Sternbilder der Erde.
Denn nur zum Rühmen noch steht mir das Herz, so gewaltig
weiß ich die Welt. Und selbst meine Klage
wird mir zur Preisung dicht vor dem stöhnenden Herzen.
Sage mir keiner, daß ich die Gegenwart nicht
liebe; ich schwinge in ihr; sie trägt mich, sie giebt mir
diesen geräumigen Tag, den uralten Werktag
daß ich ihn brauche, und wirft in gewährender Großmut
über mein Dasein niegewesene Nächte.
Ihre Hand ist stark über mir und wenn sie im Schicksal
unten mich hielte, vertaucht, ich müßte versuchen
unten zu atmen. Auch bei dem leisesten Auftrag
säng ich sie gerne. Doch vermut ich, sie will nur,
daß ich vibriere wie sie. Einst tönte der Dichter
über die Feldschlacht hinaus; was will eine Stimme
neben dem neuen Gedröhn der metallenen Handlung
drin diese Zeit sich verringt mit anstürmender Zukunft.
Auch bedarf sie des Anrufes kaum, ihr eigener Schlachtlärm
übertönt sich zum Lied. So laßt mich solange
vor Vergehendem stehn; anklagend nicht, aber
noch einmal bewundernd. Und wo mich eines
das mir vor Augen versinkt, etwa zur Klage bewegt
sei es kein Vorwurf für euch. Was sollen jüngere Völker
nicht fortstürmen von dem was der morschen oft
ruhmloser Abbruch begrub. Sehet, es wäre
arg um das Große bestellt, wenn es irgend der Schonung
bedürfte. Wem die Paläste oder der Gärten
Kühnheit nicht mehr, wem Aufstieg und Rückfall
alter Fontänen nicht mehr, wem das Verhaltene
in den Bildern oder der Statuen ewiges Dastehn
nicht mehr die Seele erschreckt und verwandelt, der gehe
diesem hinaus und tue sein Tagwerk; wo anders
lauert das Große auf ihn und wird ihn wo anders
anfalln, daß er sich wehrt.

# [FRAGMENT OF AN ELEGY]

Now shall I praise the cities, those long-surviving
(I watched them in awe) great constellations of earth.
For only in praising is my heart still mine, so violently
do I know the world. And even my lament
turns into a paean before my disconsolate heart.
Let no one say that I don't love life, the eternal
presence: I pulsate in her; she bears me, she gives me
the spaciousness of this day, the primeval workday
for me to make use of, and over my existence flings,
in her magnanimity, nights that have never been.
Her strong hand is above me, and if she should hold me
    under,
submerged in fate, I would have to learn how to breathe
down there. Even her most lightly-entrusted mission
would fill me with songs of her; although I suspect
that all she wants is for me to be vibrant as she is.
Once poets resounded over the battlefield; what voice
can outshout the rattle of this metallic age
that is struggling on toward its careening future?
And indeed it hardly requires the call, its own battle-din
roars into song. So let me stand for a while
in front of the transient: not accusing, but once again
admiring, marveling. And if perhaps something founders
before my eyes and stirs me into lament,
it is not a reproach. Why shouldn't more youthful nations
rush past the graveyard of cultures long ago rotten?
How pitiful it would be if greatness needed the slightest
indulgence. Let him whose soul is no longer startled
and transformed by palaces, by gardens' boldness, by the
    rising
and falling of ancient fountains, by everything held back
in paintings or by the infinite thereness of statues—
let such a person go out to his daily work, where
greatness is lying in ambush and someday, at some turn,
will leap upon him and force him to fight for his life.

# [URSPRÜNGLICHE FASSUNG DER ZEHNTEN ELEGIE]

*[Fragmentarisch]*

Daß ich dereinst, an dem Ausgang der grimmigen Einsicht
Jubel und Ruhm aufsinge zustimmenden Engeln.
Daß von den klar geschlagenen Hämmern des Herzens
keiner versage an weichen, zweifelnden oder
jähzornigen Saiten. Daß mich mein strömendes Antlitz
glänzender mache; daß das unscheinbare Weinen
blühe. O wie werdet ihr dann, Nächte, mir lieb sein,
gehärmte. Daß ich euch knieender nicht, untröstliche
    Schwestern,
hinnahm, nicht in euer gelöstes
Haar mich gelöster ergab. Wir Vergeuder der Schmerzen.
Wie wir sie absehn voraus in die traurige Dauer,
ob sie nicht enden vielleicht. Sie aber sind ja
Zeiten von uns, unser winter-
währiges Laubwerk, Wiesen, Teiche, angeborene
    Landschaft,
von Geschöpfen im Schilf und von Vögeln bewohnt.

Oben, der hohen, steht nicht die Hälfte der Himmel
über der Wehmut in uns, der bemühten Natur?
Denk, du beträtest nicht mehr dein verwildertes Leidtum,
sähest die Sterne nicht mehr durch das herbere Blättern
schwärzlichen Schmerzlaubs, und die Trümmer von
    Schicksal
böte dir höher nicht mehr der vergrößernde Mondschein,
daß du an ihnen dich fühlst wie ein einstiges Volk?
Lächeln auch wäre nicht mehr, das zehrende derer,
die du hinüberverlorest—, so wenig gewaltsam,
eben an dir nur vorbei, traten sie rein in dein Leid.
(Fast wie das Mädchen, das grade dem Freier sich zusprach,
der sie seit Wochen bedrängt, und sie bringt ihn erschrocken
an das Gitter des Gartens, den Mann, der frohlockt und
    ungern
fortgeht: da stört sie ein Schritt in dem neueren Abschied,

# [ORIGINAL VERSION OF THE TENTH ELEGY]

*[Fragmentary]*

Someday, emerging at last from the violent insight,
let me sing out jubilation and praise to assenting angels.
Let not even one of the clearly-struck hammers of my heart
fail to sound because of a slack, a doubtful,
or an ill-tempered string. Let my joyfully streaming face
make me more radiant; let my hidden weeping arise
and blossom. How dear you will be to me then, you nights
of anguish. Why didn't I kneel more deeply to accept you,
inconsolable sisters, and, surrendering, lose myself
in your loosened hair. How we squander our hours of pain.
How we gaze beyond them into the bitter duration
to see if they have an end. Though they are really
seasons of us, our winter-
enduring foliage, ponds, meadows, our inborn landscape,
where birds and reed-dwelling creatures are at home.

High overhead, isn't half of the night sky standing
above the sorrow in us, the disquieted garden?
Imagine that you no longer walked through your grief grown
    wild,
no longer looked at the stars through the jagged leaves
of the dark tree of pain, and the enlarging moonlight
no longer exalted fate's ruins so high
that among them you felt like the last of some ancient race.
Nor would smiles any longer exist, the consuming smiles
of those you lost over there—with so little violence,
once they were past, did they purely enter your grief.
(Almost like the girl who has just said yes to the lover
who begged her, so many weeks, and she brings him
    astonished
to the garden gate and, reluctant, he walks away,
giddy with joy; and then, amid this new parting,

und sie wartet und steht und da trifft ihr vollzähliges
    Aufschaun
ganz in das Aufschaun des Fremden, das Aufschaun der
    Jungfrau,
die ihn unendlich begreift, den draußen, der ihr bestimmt
    war,
draußen den wandernden Andern, der ihr ewig bestimmt
    war.
Hallend geht er vorbei.) So immer verlorst du;
als ein Besitzender nicht: wie sterbend einer,
vorgebeugt in die feucht herwehende Märznacht,
ach, den Frühling verliert in die Kehlen der Vögel.

Viel zu weit gehörst du in's Leiden. Vergäßest
du die geringste der maßlos erschmerzten Gestalten,
riefst du, schrieest, hoffend auf frühere Neugier,
einen der Engel herbei, der mühsam verdunkelten
    Ausdrucks
leidunmächtig, immer wieder versuchend,
dir dein Schluchzen damals, um jene, beschriebe.
Engel wie wars? Und er ahmte dir nach und verstünde
nicht daß es Schmerz sei, wie man dem rufenden Vogel
nachformt, die ihn erfüllt, die schuldlose Stimme.

a step disturbs her; she waits; and her glance in its fullness
sinks totally into a stranger's: her virgin glance
that endlessly comprehends him, the outsider, who was
    meant for her;
the wandering other, who eternally was meant for her.
Echoing, he walks by.) That is how, always, you lost:
never as one who possesses, but like someone dying
who, bending into the moist breeze of an evening in March,
loses the springtime, alas, in the throats of the birds.

Far too much you belong to grief. If you could forget her—
even the least of these figures so infinitely pained—
you would call down, shout down, hoping they might still be
    curious,
one of the angels (those beings unmighty in grief)
who, as his face darkened, would try again and again
to describe the way you kept sobbing, long ago, for her.
Angel, what was it like? And he would imitate you and never
understand that it was pain, as after a calling bird
one tries to repeat the innocent voice it is filled with.

## GEGEN-STROPHEN

Oh, daß ihr hier, Frauen, einhergeht,
hier unter uns, leidvoll,
nicht geschonter als wir und dennoch imstande,
selig zu machen wie Selige.

Woher,
wenn der Geliebte erscheint,
nehmt ihr die Zukunft?
Mehr, als je sein wird.
Wer die Entfernungen weiß
bis zum äußersten Fixstern,
staunt, wenn er diesen gewahrt,
euern herrlichen Herzraum.
Wie, im Gedräng, spart ihr ihn aus?
Ihr, voll Quellen und Nacht.

Seid ihr wirklich die gleichen,
die, da ihr Kind wart,
unwirsch im Schulgang
anstieß der ältere Bruder?
Ihr Heilen.

Wo wir als Kinder uns schon
häßlich für immer verzerrn,
wart ihr wie Brot vor der Wandlung.

Abbruch der Kindheit
war euch nicht Schaden. Auf einmal
standet ihr da, wie im Gott
plötzlich zum Wunder ergänzt.

Wir, wie gebrochen vom Berg,
oft schon als Knaben scharf
an den Rändern, vielleicht

# ANTISTROPHES

Ah, Women, that you should be moving
here, among us, grief-filled,
no more protected than we, and nevertheless
able to bless like the blessed.

From what realm,
when your beloved appears,
do you take the future?
More than will ever be.
One who knows distances
out to the outermost star
is astonished when he discovers
the magnificent space in your hearts.
How, in the crowd, can you spare it?
You, full of sources and night.

Are you really the same
as those children who
on the way to school were rudely
shoved by an older brother?
Unharmed by it.

    While we, even as children,
    disfigured ourselves forever,
    you were like bread on the altar
    before it is changed.

The breaking away of childhood
left you intact. In a moment,
you stood there, as if completed
in a miracle, all at once.

    We, as if broken from crags,
    even as boys, too sharp
    at the edges, although perhaps

manchmal glücklich behaun;
wir, wie Stücke Gesteins,
über Blumen gestürzt.

Blumen des tieferen Erdreichs,
von allen Wurzeln geliebte,
ihr, der Eurydike Schwestern,
immer voll heiliger Umkehr
hinter dem steigenden Mann.

Wir, von uns selber gekränkt,
Kränkende gern und gern
Wiedergekränkte aus Not.
Wir, wie Waffen, dem Zorn
neben den Schlaf gelegt.

Ihr, die ihr beinah Schutz seid, wo niemand
schützt. Wie ein schattiger Schlafbaum
ist der Gedanke an euch
für die Schwärme des Einsamen.

sometimes skillfully cut;
we, like pieces of rock
that have fallen on flowers.

Flowers of the deeper soil,
loved by all roots,
you, Eurydice's sisters,
full of holy return
behind the ascending man.

We, afflicted by ourselves,
gladly afflicting, gladly
needing to be afflicted.
We, who sleep with our anger
laid beside us like a knife.

You, who are almost protection
where no one protects. The thought of you
is a shade-giving tree of sleep for the restless
creatures of a solitary man.

# The Sonnets to Orpheus

## (1923)

*Written as a grave-monument*
*for Vera Ouckama Knoop*

*Château de Muzot, February 1922*

## ERSTER TEIL

I

Da stieg ein Baum. O reine Übersteigung!
O Orpheus singt! O hoher Baum im Ohr!
Und alles schwieg. Doch selbst in der Verschweigung
ging neuer Anfang, Wink und Wandlung vor.

Tiere aus Stille drangen aus dem klaren
gelösten Wald von Lager und Genist;
und da ergab sich, daß sie nicht aus List
und nicht aus Angst in sich so leise waren,

sondern aus Hören. Brüllen, Schrei, Geröhr
schien klein in ihren Herzen. Und wo eben
kaum eine Hütte war, dies zu empfangen,

ein Unterschlupf aus dunkelstem Verlangen
mit einem Zugang, dessen Pfosten beben,—
da schufst du ihnen Tempel im Gehör.

# FIRST PART

---

## I

A tree ascended there. Oh pure transcendence!
Oh Orpheus sings! Oh tall tree in the ear!
And all things hushed. Yet even in that silence
a new beginning, beckoning, change appeared.

Creatures of stillness crowded from the bright
unbound forest, out of their lairs and nests;
and it was not from any dullness, not
from fear, that they were so quiet in themselves,

but from just listening. Bellow, roar, shriek
seemed small inside their hearts. And where there had been
at most a makeshift hut to receive the music,

a shelter nailed up out of their darkest longing,
with an entryway that shuddered in the wind—
you built a temple deep inside their hearing.

## II

Und fast ein Mädchen wars und ging hervor
aus diesem einigen Glück von Sang und Leier
und glänzte klar durch ihre Frühlingsschleier
und machte sich ein Bett in meinem Ohr.

Und schlief in mir. Und alles war ihr Schlaf.
Die Bäume, die ich je bewundert, diese
fühlbare Ferne, die gefühlte Wiese
und jedes Staunen, das mich selbst betraf.

Sie schlief die Welt. Singender Gott, wie hast
du sie vollendet, daß sie nicht begehrte,
erst wach zu sein? Sieh, sie erstand und schlief.

Wo ist ihr Tod? O, wirst du dies Motiv
erfinden noch, eh sich dein Lied verzehrte?—
Wo sinkt sie hin aus mir? . . . Ein Mädchen fast . . . .

# II

And it was almost a girl and came to be
out of this single joy of song and lyre
and through her green veils shone forth radiantly
and made herself a bed inside my ear.

And slept there. And her sleep was everything:
the awesome trees, the distances I had felt
so deeply that I could touch them, meadows in spring:
all wonders that had ever seized my heart.

She slept the world. Singing god, how was that first
sleep so perfect that she had no desire
ever to wake? See: she arose and slept.

Where is her death now? Ah, will you discover
this theme before your song consumes itself?—
Where is she vanishing? . . . A girl almost . . . .

## III

Ein Gott vermags. Wie aber, sag mir, soll
ein Mann ihm folgen durch die schmale Leier?
Sein Sinn ist Zwiespalt. An der Kreuzung zweier
Herzwege steht kein Tempel für Apoll.

Gesang, wie du ihn lehrst, ist nicht Begehr,
nicht Werbung um ein endlich noch Erreichtes;
Gesang ist Dasein. Für den Gott ein Leichtes.
Wann aber *sind* wir? Und wann wendet *er*

an unser Sein die Erde und die Sterne?
Dies *ists* nicht, Jüngling, daß du liebst, wenn auch
die Stimme dann den Mund dir aufstößt,—lerne

vergessen, daß du aufsangst. Das verrinnt.
In Wahrheit singen, ist ein andrer Hauch.
Ein Hauch um nichts. Ein Wehn im Gott. Ein Wind.

# III

A god can do it. But will you tell me how
a man can enter through the lyre's strings?
Our mind is split. And at the shadowed crossing
of heart-roads, there is no temple for Apollo.

Song, as you have taught it, is not desire,
not wooing any grace that can be achieved;
song is reality. Simple, for a god.
But when can *we* be real? When does he pour

the earth, the stars, into us? Young man,
it is not your loving, even if your mouth
was forced wide open by your own voice—learn

to forget that passionate music. It will end.
True singing is a different breath, about
nothing. A gust inside the god. A wind.

## IV

O ihr Zärtlichen, tretet zuweilen
in den Atem, der euch nicht meint,
laßt ihn an eueren Wangen sich teilen,
hinter euch zittert er, wieder vereint.

O ihr Seligen, o ihr Heilen,
die ihr der Anfang der Herzen scheint.
Bogen der Pfeile und Ziele von Pfeilen,
ewiger glänzt euer Lächeln verweint.

Fürchtet euch nicht zu leiden, die Schwere,
gebt sie zurück an der Erde Gewicht;
schwer sind die Berge, schwer sind die Meere.

Selbst die als Kinder ihr pflanztet, die Bäume,
wurden zu schwer längst; ihr trüget sie nicht.
Aber die Lüfte . . . aber die Räume . . . .

# IV

O you tender ones, walk now and then
into the breath that blows coldly past.
Upon your cheeks let it tremble and part;
behind you it will tremble together again.

O you blessèd ones, you who are whole,
you who seem the beginning of hearts,
bows for the arrows and arrows' targets—
tear-bright, your lips more eternally smile.

Don't be afraid to suffer; return
that heaviness to the earth's own weight;
heavy are the mountains, heavy the seas.

Even the small trees you planted as children
have long since become too heavy; you could not
carry them now. But the winds . . . But the spaces . . . .

## V

Errichtet keinen Denkstein. Laßt die Rose
nur jedes Jahr zu seinen Gunsten blühn.
Denn Orpheus ists. Seine Metamorphose
in dem und dem. Wir sollen uns nicht mühn

um andre Namen. Ein für alle Male
ists Orpheus, wenn es singt. Er kommt und geht.
Ists nicht schon viel, wenn er die Rosenschale
um ein paar Tage manchmal übersteht?

O wie er schwinden muß, daß ihrs begrifft!
Und wenn ihm selbst auch bangte, daß er schwände.
Indem sein Wort das Hiersein übertrifft,

ist er schon dort, wohin ihrs nicht begleitet.
Der Leier Gitter zwängt ihm nicht die Hände.
Und er gehorcht, indem er überschreitet.

# V

Erect no gravestone for him. Only this:
let the rose blossom each year for his sake.
For it *is* the god. His metamorphosis
in this and that. We do not need to look

for other names. It is Orpheus once for all
whenever there is song. He comes and goes.
Isn't it enough if sometimes he can dwell
with us a few days longer than a rose?

Though he himself is afraid to disappear,
he *has* to vanish: don't you understand?
The moment his word moves out beyond our life here,

he has gone where you will never find his trace.
The lyre's strings do not constrict his hands.
And it is in overstepping that he obeys.

## VI

Ist er ein Hiesiger? Nein, aus beiden
Reichen erwuchs seine weite Natur.
Kundiger böge die Zweige der Weiden,
wer die Wurzeln der Weiden erfuhr.

Geht ihr zu Bette, so laßt auf dem Tische
Brot nicht und Milch nicht; die Toten ziehts—.
Aber er, der Beschwörende, mische
unter der Milde des Augenlids

ihre Erscheinung in alles Geschaute;
und der Zauber von Erdrauch und Raute
sei ihm so wahr wie der klarste Bezug.

Nichts kann das gültige Bild ihm verschlimmern;
sei es aus Gräbern, sei es aus Zimmern,
rühme er Fingerring, Spange und Krug.

# VI

Is he someone who dwells in this *single* world? No:
both realms are the source of his earthly power.
He alone who has known the roots of the willow
can bend the willow-branch into a lyre.

Overnight leave no bread on the table
and leave no milk: they draw back the dead—.
But he, the conjuror, may he settle
under the calm of the eye's lowered lid

to mix death into everything seen;
and may the magic of earthsmoke and rue
be as real to him as the clearest connection.

Nothing can trouble the dominance of
the true image. Whether from graves or from rooms,
let him praise finger-ring, bracelet, and jug.

## VII

Rühmen, das ists! Ein zum Rühmen Bestellter,
ging er hervor wie das Erz aus des Steins
Schweigen. Sein Herz, o vergängliche Kelter
eines den Menschen unendlichen Weins.

Nie versagt ihm die Stimme am Staube,
wenn ihn das göttliche Beispiel ergreift.
Alles wird Weinberg, alles wird Traube,
in seinem fühlenden Süden gereift.

Nicht in den Grüften der Könige Moder
straft ihm die Rühmung lügen, oder
daß von den Göttern ein Schatten fällt.

Er ist einer der bleibenden Boten,
der noch weit in die Türen der Toten
Schalen mit rühmlichen Früchten hält.

# VII

Praising is what matters! He was summoned for that,
and came to us like the ore from a stone's
silence. His mortal heart presses out
a deathless, inexhaustible wine.

Whenever he feels the god's paradigm grip
his throat, the voice does not die in his mouth.
All becomes vineyard, all becomes grape,
ripened on the hills of his sensuous South.

Neither decay in the sepulcher of kings
nor any shadow fallen from the gods
can ever detract from his glorious praising.

For he is a herald who is with us always,
holding far into the doors of the dead
a bowl with ripe fruit worthy of praise.

## VIII

Nur im Raum der Rühmung darf die Klage
gehn, die Nymphe des geweinten Quells,
wachend über unserm Niederschlage,
daß er klar sei an demselben Fels,

der die Tore trägt und die Altäre.—
Sieh, um ihre stillen Schultern früht
das Gefühl, daß sie die jüngste wäre
unter den Geschwistern im Gemüt.

Jubel *weiß*, und Sehnsucht ist geständig,—
nur die Klage lernt noch; mädchenhändig
zählt sie nächtelang das alte Schlimme.

Aber plötzlich, schräg und ungeübt,
hält sie doch ein Sternbild unsrer Stimme
in den Himmel, den ihr Hauch nicht trübt.

# VIII

Only in the realm of Praising should Lament
walk, the naiad of the wept-for fountain,
watching over the stream of our complaint,
to keep it clear upon the very stone

that bears the arch of triumph and the altar.—
Look: around her shoulders dawns the bright
sense that she may be the youngest sister
among the deities hidden in our heart.

Joy *knows*, and Longing has accepted—
only Lament still learns; upon her beads,
night after night, she counts the ancient curse.

Yet awkward as she is, she suddenly
lifts a constellation of our voice,
glittering, into the pure nocturnal sky.

## IX

Nur wer die Leier schon hob
auch unter Schatten,
darf das unendliche Lob
ahnend erstatten.

Nur wer mit Toten vom Mohn
aß, von dem ihren,
wird nicht den leisesten Ton
wieder verlieren.

Mag auch die Spieglung im Teich
oft uns verschwimmen:
*Wisse das Bild*.

Erst in dem Doppelbereich
werden die Stimmen
ewig und mild.

# IX

Only he whose bright lyre
has sounded in shadows
may, looking onward, restore
his infinite praise.

Only he who has eaten
poppies with the dead
will not lose ever again
the gentlest chord.

Though the image upon the pool
often grows dim:
*Know and be still.*

Inside the Double World
all voices become
eternally mild.

## X

Euch, die ihr nie mein Gefühl verließt,
grüß ich, antikische Sarkophage,
die das fröhliche Wasser römischer Tage
als ein wandelndes Lied durchfließt.

Oder jene so offenen, wie das Aug
eines frohen erwachenden Hirten,
—innen voll Stille und Bienensaug—
denen entzückte Falter entschwirrten;

alle, die man dem Zweifel entreißt,
grüß ich, die wiedergeöffneten Munde,
die schon wußten, was schweigen heißt.

Wissen wirs, Freunde, wissen wirs nicht?
Beides bildet die zögernde Stunde
in dem menschlichen Angesicht.

# X

You who are close to my heart always,
I welcome you, ancient coffins of stone,
which the cheerful water of Roman days
still flows through, like a wandering song.

Or those other ones that are open wide
like the eyes of a happily waking shepherd
—with silence and bee-suck nettle inside,
from which ecstatic butterflies flittered;

everything that has been wrestled from doubt
I welcome—the mouths that burst open after
long knowledge of what it is to be mute.

Do we know this, my friends, or don't we know this?
Both are formed by the hesitant hour
in the deep calm of the human face.

## XI

Sieh den Himmel. Heißt kein Sternbild 'Reiter'?
Denn dies ist uns seltsam eingeprägt:
dieser Stolz aus Erde. Und ein Zweiter,
der ihn treibt und hält und den er trägt.

Ist nicht so, gejagt und dann gebändigt,
diese sehnige Natur des Seins?
Weg und Wendung. Doch ein Druck verständigt.
Neue Weite. Und die zwei sind eins.

Aber *sind* sie's? Oder meinen beide
nicht den Weg, den sie zusammen tun?
Namenlos schon trennt sie Tisch und Weide.

Auch die sternische Verbindung trügt.
Doch uns freue eine Weile nun
der Figur zu glauben. Das genügt.

# XI

Look at the sky. Are no two stars called "Rider"?
For this is printed strangely on us here:
this pride of earth. And look, the second figure
who drives and halts it: whom it has to bear.

Aren't we, in our sinewy quintessence,
controlled like this, now raced and now reined in?
Path and turningpoint. Just a touch possesses.
New expanses. And the two are one.

Or *are* they really? Don't both signify
the path they ride together now? But table
and pasture keep them separate, utterly.

Even the starry union is a fraud.
Yet gladly let us trust the valid symbol
for a moment. It is all we need.

## XII

Heil dem Geist, der uns verbinden mag;
denn wir leben wahrhaft in Figuren.
Und mit kleinen Schritten gehn die Uhren
neben unserm eigentlichen Tag.

Ohne unsern wahren Platz zu kennen,
handeln wir aus wirklichem Bezug.
Die Antennen fühlen die Antennen,
und die leere Ferne trug . . .

Reine Spannung. O Musik der Kräfte!
Ist nicht durch die läßlichen Geschäfte
jede Störung von dir abgelenkt?

Selbst wenn sich der Bauer sorgt und handelt,
wo die Saat in Sommer sich verwandelt,
reicht er niemals hin. Die Erde *schenkt*.

## XII

Hail to the god who joins us; for through him
arise the symbols where we truly live.
And, with tiny footsteps, the clocks move
separately from our authentic time.

Though we are unaware of our true status,
our actions stem from pure relationship.
Far away, antennas hear antennas
and the empty distances transmit . . .

Pure readiness. Oh unheard starry music!
Isn't your sound protected from all static
by the ordinary business of our days?

In spite of all the farmer's work and worry,
he can't reach down to where the seed is slowly
transmuted into summer. The earth *bestows*.

## XIII

Voller Apfel, Birne und Banane,
Stachelbeere . . . Alles dieses spricht
Tod und Leben in den Mund . . . Ich ahne . . .
Lest es einem Kind vom Angesicht,

wenn es sie erschmeckt. Dies kommt von weit.
Wird euch langsam namenlos im Munde?
Wo sonst Worte waren, fließen Funde,
aus dem Fruchtfleisch überrascht befreit.

Wagt zu sagen, was ihr Apfel nennt.
Diese Süße, die sich erst verdichtet,
um, im Schmecken leise aufgerichtet,

klar zu werden, wach und transparent,
doppeldeutig, sonnig, erdig, hiesig—:
O Erfahrung, Fühlung, Freude—, riesig!

# XIII

Plump apple, smooth banana, melon, peach,
gooseberry . . . How all this affluence
speaks death and life into the mouth . . . I sense . . .
Observe it from a child's transparent features

while he tastes. This comes from far away.
What miracle is happening in your mouth?
Instead of words, discoveries flow out
from the ripe flesh, astonished to be free.

Dare to say what "apple" truly is.
This sweetness that feels thick, dark, dense at first;
then, exquisitely lifted in your taste,

grows clarified, awake and luminous,
double-meaninged, sunny, earthy, real—:
Oh knowledge, pleasure—inexhaustible.

## XIV

Wir gehen um mit Blume, Weinblatt, Frucht.
Sie sprechen nicht die Sprache nur des Jahres.
Aus Dunkel steigt ein buntes Offenbares
und hat vielleicht den Glanz der Eifersucht

der Toten an sich, die die Erde stärken.
Was wissen wir von ihrem Teil an dem?
Es ist seit lange ihre Art, den Lehm
mit ihrem freien Marke zu durchmärken.

Nun fragt sich nur: tun sie es gern? . . .
Drängt diese Frucht, ein Werk von schweren Sklaven,
geballt zu uns empor, zu ihren Herrn?

Sind *sie* die Herrn, die bei den Wurzeln schlafen,
und gönnen uns aus ihren Überflüssen
dies Zwischending aus stummer Kraft und Küssen?

## XIV

We are involved with flower, leaf, and fruit.
They speak not just the language of one year.
From darkness a bright phenomenon appears
and still reflects, perhaps, the jealous glint

of the dead, who fill the earth. How can we know
what part they play within the ancient cycle?
Long since, it has been their job to make the soil
vigorous with the force of their free marrow.

But have they done it willingly? we ask . . .
Does this fruit, formed by heavy slaves, push up
like a clenched fist, to threaten us, their masters?

Or in fact are *they* the masters, as they sleep
beside the roots and grant us, from their riches,
this hybrid Thing of speechless strength and kisses?

## XV

Wartet . . . , das schmeckt . . . Schon ists auf der Flucht.
. . . . Wenig Musik nur, ein Stampfen, ein Summen—:
Mädchen, ihr warmen, Mädchen, ihr stummen,
tanzt den Geschmack der erfahrenen Frucht!

Tanzt die Orange. Wer kann sie vergessen,
wie sie, ertrinkend in sich, sich wehrt
wider ihr Süßsein. Ihr habt sie besessen.
Sie hat sich köstlich zu euch bekehrt.

Tanzt die Orange. Die wärmere Landschaft,
werft sie aus euch, daß die reife erstrahle
in Lüften der Heimat! Erglühte, enthüllt

Düfte um Düfte. Schafft die Verwandtschaft
mit der reinen, sich weigernden Schale,
mit dem Saft, der die Glückliche füllt!

## XV

Wait . . . , that tastes good . . . But already it's gone.
. . . . A few notes of music, a tapping, a faint
hum—: you girls, so warm and so silent,
dance the taste of the fruit you have known!

Dance the orange. Who can forget it,
drowning in itself, how it struggles through
against its own sweetness. You have possessed it.
Deliciously it has converted to you.

Dance the orange. The sunnier landscape—
fling it *from* you, allow it to shine
in the breeze of its homeland! Aglow, peel away

scent after scent. Create your own kinship
with the supple, gently reluctant rind
and the juice that fills it with succulent joy.

## XVI

Du, mein Freund, bist einsam, weil . . . .
*Wir* machen mit Worten und Fingerzeigen
uns allmählich die Welt zu eigen,
vielleicht ihren schwächsten, gefährlichsten Teil.

Wer zeigt mit Fingern auf einen Geruch?—
Doch von den Kräften, die uns bedrohten,
fühlst du viele . . . Du kennst die Toten,
und du erschrickst vor dem Zauberspruch.

Sieh, nun heißt es zusammen ertragen
Stückwerk und Teile, als sei es das Ganze.
Dir helfen, wird schwer sein. Vor allem: pflanze

mich nicht in dein Herz. Ich wüchse zu schnell.
Doch *meines* Herrn Hand will ich führen und sagen:
Hier. Das ist Esau in seinem Fell.

## XVI

You are lonely, my friend, because you are . . . .
*We,* with a word or a finger-sign,
gradually make the world our own,
though perhaps its weakest, most precarious part.

How can fingers point out a smell?—
Yet of the dark forces that lurk at our side
you feel many . . . You know the dead,
and you shrink away from the magic spell.

Look, we two together must bear
piecework and parts, as if they were
the whole. But be careful. Above all, don't plant

me inside your heart. I'd outgrow you. But I
will guide *my* master's hand and will say:
Here. This is Esau beneath his pelt.

## XVII

Zu unterst der Alte, verworrn,
all der Erbauten
Wurzel, verborgener Born,
den sie nie schauten.

Sturmhelm und Jägerhorn,
Spruch von Ergrauten,
Männer im Bruderzorn,
Frauen wie Lauten . . .

Drängender Zweig an Zweig,
nirgends ein freier . . . .
Einer! O steig . . . o steig . . .

Aber sie brechen noch.
Dieser erst oben doch
biegt sich zur Leier.

## XVII

At bottom the Ancient One, gnarled
root hidden deep,
origin unbeheld
by those who branched up.

Helmet and horn of hunters,
grandfathers' truths,
men who betrayed their brothers,
women like lutes . . .

Branch upon branch crowds close,
none of them free . . . .
Keep climbing higher . . . higher . . .

Still, though, they break. Yet this
top one bends finally
into a lyre.

## XVIII

Hörst du das Neue, Herr,
dröhnen und beben?
Kommen Verkündiger,
die es erheben.

Zwar ist kein Hören heil
in dem Durchtobtsein,
doch der Maschinenteil
will jetzt gelobt sein.

Sieh, die Maschine:
wie sie sich wälzt und rächt
und uns entstellt und schwächt.

Hat sie aus uns auch Kraft,
sie, ohne Leidenschaft,
treibe und diene.

## XVIII

Master, do you hear the New
quiver and rumble?
Harbingers step forth who
blare their approval.

Surely no ear is whole
amid this noise,
yet the machine-part still
asks for our praise.

Look, the machine:
rears up and takes revenge,
brings us to crawl and cringe.

Since all its strength is from us,
let it, desireless,
serve and remain.

## XIX

Wandelt sich rasch auch die Welt
wie Wolkengestalten,
alles Vollendete fällt
heim zum Uralten.

Über dem Wandel und Gang,
weiter und freier,
währt noch dein Vor-Gesang,
Gott mit der Leier.

Nicht sind die Leiden erkannt,
nicht ist die Liebe gelernt,
und was im Tod uns entfernt,

ist nicht entschleiert.
Einzig das Lied überm Land
heiligt und feiert.

# XIX

Though the world keeps changing its form
as fast as a cloud, still
what is accomplished falls home
to the Primeval.

Over the change and the passing,
larger and freer,
soars your eternal song,
god with the lyre.

Never has grief been possessed,
never has love been learned,
and what removes us in death

is not revealed.
Only the song through the land
hallows and heals.

## XX

Dir aber, Herr, o was weih ich dir, sag,
der das Ohr den Geschöpfen gelehrt?—
Mein Erinnern an einen Frühlingstag,
seinen Abend, in Rußland—, ein Pferd . . .

Herüber vom Dorf kam der Schimmel allein,
an der vorderen Fessel den Pflock,
um die Nacht auf den Wiesen allein zu sein;
wie schlug seiner Mähne Gelock

an den Hals im Takte des Übermuts,
bei dem grob gehemmten Galopp.
Wie sprangen die Quellen des Rossebluts!

Der fühlte die Weiten, und ob!
Der sang und der hörte—, dein Sagenkreis
war *in* ihm geschlossen.

                    Sein Bild: ich weih's.

## XX

But Master, what gift shall I dedicate to you,
who taught all creatures their ears?
—My thoughts of an evening long ago,
it was springtime, in Russia—a horse . . .

He came bounding from the village, alone, white,
with a hobble attached to one leg,
to stay alone in the fields all night;
how the mane beat against his neck

to the rhythm of his perfect joy, in that hindered
gallop across the meadow.
What leaping went on in his stallion-blood!

He felt the expanses, and oh!
He sang and he heard—your cycle of myths
was completed *in* him.
His image: my gift.

## XXI

Frühling ist wiedergekommen. Die Erde
ist wie ein Kind, das Gedichte weiß;
viele, o viele . . . . Für die Beschwerde
langen Lernens bekommt sie den Preis.

Streng war ihr Lehrer. Wir mochten das Weiße
an dem Barte des alten Manns.
Nun, wie das Grüne, das Blaue heiße,
dürfen wir fragen: sie kanns, sie kanns!

Erde, die frei hat, du glückliche, spiele
nun mit den Kindern. Wir wollen dich fangen,
fröhliche Erde. Dem Frohsten gelingts.

O, was der Lehrer sie lehrte, das Viele,
und was gedruckt steht in Wurzeln und langen
schwierigen Stämmen: sie singts, sie singts!

# XXI

Spring has returned. The earth resembles
a little girl who has memorized
many poems . . . . For all the trouble
of her long learning, she wins the prize.

Her teacher was strict. We loved the white
in the old man's beard and shaggy eyebrows.
Now, whatever we ask about
the blue and the green, she knows, she knows!

Earth, overjoyed to be out on vacation,
play with the children. We long to catch up,
jubilant Earth. The happiest will win.

What her teacher taught her, the numberless Things,
and what lies hidden in stem and in deep
difficult root, she sings, she sings!

## XXII

Wir sind die Treibenden.
Aber den Schritt der Zeit,
nehmt ihn als Kleinigkeit
im immer Bleibenden.

Alles das Eilende
wird schon vorüber sein;
denn das Verweilende
erst weiht uns ein.

Knaben, o werft den Mut
nicht in die Schnelligkeit,
nicht in den Flugversuch.

Alles ist ausgeruht:
Dunkel und Helligkeit,
Blume und Buch.

## XXII

We are the driving ones.
Ah, but the step of time:
think of it as a dream
in what forever remains.

All that is hurrying
soon will be over with;
only what lasts can bring
us to the truth.

Young men, don't put your trust
into the trials of flight,
into the hot and quick.

All things already rest:
darkness and morning light,
flower and book.

## XXIII

O erst *dann*, wenn der Flug
nicht mehr um seinetwillen
wird in die Himmelstillen
steigen, sich selber genug,

um in lichten Profilen,
als das Gerät, das gelang,
Liebling der Winde zu spielen,
sicher, schwenkend und schlank,—

erst, wenn ein reines Wohin
wachsender Apparate
Knabenstolz überwiegt,

wird, überstürzt von Gewinn,
jener den Fernen Genahte
*sein*, was er einsam erfliegt.

## XXIII

Not till the day when flight
no longer for its own sake ascends
into the silent heavens
propelled by its self-conceit,

so that, in luminous outlines,
as the tool that has come to power,
it can float, caressed by the winds,
streamlined, agile, and sure—

not till a pure destination
outweighs the boyish boast
of how much machines can do

will, overwhelmed with gain,
one to whom distance is close
*be* what alone he flew.

## XXIV

Sollen wir unsere uralte Freundschaft, die großen
niemals werbenden Götter, weil sie der harte
Stahl, den wir streng erzogen, nicht kennt, verstoßen
oder sie plötzlich suchen auf einer Karte?

Diese gewaltigen Freunde, die uns die Toten
nehmen, rühren nirgends an unsere Räder.
Unsere Gastmähler haben wir weit—, unsere Bäder,
fortgerückt, und ihre uns lang schon zu langsamen Boten

überholen wir immer. Einsamer nun auf einander
ganz angewiesen, ohne einander zu kennen,
führen wir nicht mehr die Pfade als schöne Mäander,

sondern als Grade. Nur noch in Dampfkesseln brennen
die einstigen Feuer und heben die Hämmer, die immer
größern. Wir aber nehmen an Kraft ab, wie Schwimmer.

## XXIV

Shall we reject our primordial friendship, the sublime
unwooing gods, because the steel that we keep
harshly bringing to hardness has never known them—
or shall we suddenly look for them on a map?

All these powerful friends, who withdraw the dead
from the reach of the senses, touch nowhere against our
    wheels.
We have moved our banquets, our baths and our festivals,
far away. And their messengers, long since outstripped by
    our speed,

have vanished. Lonelier now, dependent on one another
utterly, though not knowing one another at all,
we no longer lay out each path as a lovely meander,

but straight ahead. Only in factories do the once-consecrate
    flames still
burn and lift up the always heavier hammers.
We, though, keep losing what small strength we have, like
    swimmers.

## XXV

*Dich* aber will ich nun, *Dich,* die ich kannte
wie eine Blume, von der ich den Namen nicht weiß,
noch *ein* Mal erinnern und ihnen zeigen, Entwandte,
schöne Gespielin des unüberwindlichen Schrei's.

Tänzerin erst, die plötzlich, den Körper voll Zögern,
anhielt, als göß man ihr Jungsein in Erz;
trauernd und lauschend—. Da, von den hohen Vermögern
fiel ihr Musik in das veränderte Herz.

Nah war die Krankheit. Schon von den Schatten bemächtigt,
drängte verdunkelt das Blut, doch, wie flüchtig verdächtigt,
trieb es in seinen natürlichen Frühling hervor.

Wieder und wieder, von Dunkel und Sturz unterbrochen,
glänzte es irdisch. Bis es nach schrecklichem Pochen
trat in das trostlos offene Tor.

## XXV

But you now, dear girl, whom I loved like a flower whose
    name
I didn't know, you who so early were taken away:
I will once more call up your image and show it to them,
beautiful companion of the unsubduable cry.

Dancer whose body filled with your hesitant fate,
pausing, as though your young flesh had been cast in bronze;
grieving and listening—. Then, from the high dominions,
unearthly music fell into your altered heart.

Already possessed by shadows, with illness near,
your blood flowed darkly; yet, though for a moment
    suspicious,
it burst out into the natural pulses of spring.

Again and again interrupted by downfall and darkness,
earthly, it gleamed. Till, after a terrible pounding,
it entered the inconsolably open door.

## XXVI

Du aber, Göttlicher, du, bis zuletzt noch Ertöner,
da ihn der Schwarm der verschmähten Mänaden befiel,
hast ihr Geschrei übertönt mit Ordnung, du Schöner,
aus den Zerstörenden stieg dein erbauendes Spiel.

Keine war da, daß sie Haupt dir und Leier zerstör.
Wie sie auch rangen und rasten, und alle die scharfen
Steine, die sie nach deinem Herzen warfen,
wurden zu Sanftem an dir und begabt mit Gehör.

Schließlich zerschlugen sie dich, von der Rache gehetzt,
während dein Klang noch in Löwen und Felsen verweilte
und in den Bäumen und Vögeln. Dort singst du noch jetzt.

O du verlorener Gott! Du unendliche Spur!
Nur weil dich reißend zuletzt die Feindschaft verteilte,
sind wir die Hörenden jetzt und ein Mund der Natur.

# XXVI

But you, divine poet, you who sang on till the end
as the swarm of rejected maenads attacked you, shrieking,
you overpowered their noise with harmony, and
from pure destruction arose your transfigured song.

Their hatred could not destroy your head or your lyre,
however they wrestled and raged; and each one of the sharp
stones that they hurled, vengeance-crazed, at your heart
softened while it was in mid-flight, enchanted to hear.

At last they killed you and broke you in pieces while
your sound kept lingering on in lions and boulders,
in trees and in birds. There you are singing still.

Oh you lost god! You inexhaustible trace!
Only because you were torn and scattered through Nature
have *we* become hearers now and a rescuing voice.

## ZWEITER TEIL

I

Atmen, du unsichtbares Gedicht!
Immerfort um das eigne
Sein rein eingetauschter Weltraum. Gegengewicht,
in dem ich mich rhythmisch ereigne.

Einzige Welle, deren
allmähliches Meer ich bin;
sparsamstes du von allen möglichen Meeren,—
Raumgewinn.

Wieviele von diesen Stellen der Räume waren schon
innen in mir. Manche Winde
sind wie mein Sohn.

Erkennst du mich, Luft, du, voll noch einst meiniger Orte?
Du, einmal glatte Rinde,
Rundung und Blatt meiner Worte.

# SECOND PART

## I

Breathing: you invisible poem! Complete
interchange of our own
essence with world-space. You counterweight
in which I rhythmically happen.

Single wave-motion whose
gradual sea I am;
you, most inclusive of all our possible seas—
space grown warm.

How many regions in space have already been
inside me. There are winds that seem like
my wandering son.

Do you recognize me, air, full of places I once absorbed?
You who were the smooth bark,
roundness, and leaf of my words.

## II

So wie dem Meister manchmal das eilig
nähere Blatt den *wirklichen* Strich
abnimmt: so nehmen oft Spiegel das heilig
einzige Lächeln der Mädchen in sich,

wenn sie den Morgen erproben, allein,—
oder im Glanze der dienenden Lichter.
Und in das Atmen der echten Gesichter,
später, fällt nur ein Widerschein.

*Was* haben Augen einst ins umrußte
lange Verglühn der Kamine geschaut:
Blicke des Lebens, für immer verlorne.

Ach, der Erde, wer kennt die Verluste?
Nur, wer mit dennoch preisendem Laut
sänge das Herz, das ins Ganze geborne.

# II

Just as the master's *genuine* brushstroke
is sometimes caught by a hurried page
that happens to be there: so mirrors will take
into themselves the pure smiling image

of girls as they test the morning, alone—
or under the gleam of devoted candles.
And into their faces, one by one,
later, just a reflection falls.

*How much* was once gazed into the charred
slow-dying glow of a fireplace:
glances of life, irretrievable.

Who knows what losses the earth has suffered?
One who, with sounds that nonetheless praise,
can sing the heart born into the whole.

## III

Spiegel: noch nie hat man wissend beschrieben,
was ihr in euerem Wesen seid.
Ihr, wie mit lauter Löchern von Sieben
erfüllten Zwischenräume der Zeit.

Ihr, noch des leeren Saales Verschwender—,
wenn es dämmert, wie Wälder weit . . .
Und der Lüster geht wie ein Sechzehn-Ender
durch eure Unbetretbarkeit.

Manchmal seid ihr voll Malerei.
Einige scheinen *in* euch gegangen—,
andere schicktet ihr scheu vorbei.

Aber die Schönste wird bleiben—, bis
drüben in ihre enthaltenen Wangen
eindrang der klare gelöste Narziß.

## III

Mirrors: no one has ever known how
to describe what you are in your inmost realm.
As if filled with nothing but sieve-holes, you
fathomless in-between spaces of time.

You prodigals of the empty chamber—
vast as forests, at the close of day . . .
And the chandelier strides like a sixteen-pointer
through your unenterability.

Sometimes you are full of painting. A few
seem to have walked straight into your depths—
others, shyly, you sent on past you.

But the loveliest will stay—until, beyond,
into her all-absorbed cheeks she lets
Narcissus penetrate, bright and unbound.

## IV

O dieses ist das Tier, das es nicht giebt.
Sie wußtens nicht und habens jeden Falls
—sein Wandeln, seine Haltung, seinen Hals,
bis in des stillen Blickes Licht—geliebt.

Zwar *war* es nicht. Doch weil sie's liebten, ward
ein reines Tier. Sie ließen immer Raum.
Und in dem Raume, klar und ausgespart,
erhob es leicht sein Haupt und brauchte kaum

zu sein. Sie nährten es mit keinem Korn,
nur immer mit der Möglichkeit, es sei.
Und die gab solche Stärke an das Tier,

daß es aus sich ein Stirnhorn trieb. Ein Horn.
Zu einer Jungfrau kam es weiß herbei—
und war im Silber-Spiegel und in ihr.

# IV

Oh this beast is the one that never was.
They didn't know that; unconcerned, they had
loved its grace, its walk, and how it stood
looking at them calmly, with clear eyes.

It hadn't *been*. But from their love, a pure
beast arose. They always left it room.
And in that heart-space, radiant and bare,
it raised its head and hardly needed to

exist. They fed it, not with any grain,
but always just with the thought that it might be.
And this assurance gave the beast so much power,

it grew a horn upon its brow. One horn.
Afterward it approached a virgin, whitely—
and was, inside the mirror and in her.

## V

Blumenmuskel, der der Anemone
Wiesenmorgen nach und nach erschließt,
bis in ihren Schooß das polyphone
Licht der lauten Himmel sich ergießt,

in den stillen Blütenstern gespannter
Muskel des unendlichen Empfangs,
manchmal *so* von Fülle übermannter,
daß der Ruhewink des Untergangs

kaum vermag die weitzurückgeschnellten
Blätterränder dir zurückzugeben:
du, Entschluß und Kraft von *wie*viel Welten!

Wir, Gewaltsamen, wir währen länger.
Aber *wann,* in welchem aller Leben,
sind wir endlich offen und Empfänger?

V

Flower-muscle that slowly opens back
the anemone to another meadow-dawn,
until her womb can feel the polyphonic
light of the sonorous heavens pouring down;

muscle of an infinite acceptance,
stretched within the silent blossom-star,
at times *so* overpowered with abundance
that sunset's signal for repose is bare-

ly able to return your too far hurled-
back petals for the darkness to revive:
you, strength and purpose of how many worlds!

We violent ones remain a little longer.
Ah but *when*, in which of all our lives,
shall we at last be open and receivers?

## VI

Rose, du thronende, denen im Altertume
warst du ein Kelch mit einfachem Rand.
*Uns* aber bist du die volle zahllose Blume,
der unerschöpfliche Gegenstand.

In deinem Reichtum scheinst du wie Kleidung um Kleidung
um einen Leib aus nichts als Glanz;
aber dein einzelnes Blatt ist zugleich die Vermeidung
und die Verleugnung jedes Gewands.

Seit Jahrhunderten ruft uns dein Duft
seine süßesten Namen herüber;
plötzlich liegt er wie Ruhm in der Luft.

Dennoch, wir wissen ihn nicht zu nennen, wir raten . . .
Und Erinnerung geht zu ihm über,
die wir von rufbaren Stunden erbaten.

# VI

Rose, you majesty—once, to the ancients, you were
just a calyx with the simplest of rims.
But for us, you are the full, the numberless flower,
the inexhaustible countenance.

In your wealth you seem to be wearing gown upon gown
upon a body of nothing but light;
yet each separate petal is at the same time the negation
of all clothing and the refusal of it.

Your fragrance has been calling its sweetest names
in our direction, for hundreds of years;
suddenly it hangs in the air like fame.

Even so, we have never known what to call it; we guess . . .
And memory is filled with it unawares
which we prayed for from hours that belong to us.

## VII

Blumen, ihr schließlich den ordnenden Händen verwandte,
(Händen der Mädchen von einst und jetzt),
die auf dem Gartentisch oft von Kante zu Kante
lagen, ermattet und sanft verletzt,

wartend des Wassers, das sie noch einmal erhole
aus dem begonnenen Tod—, und nun
wieder erhobene zwischen die strömenden Pole
fühlender Finger, die wohlzutun

mehr noch vermögen, als ihr ahntet, ihr leichten,
wenn ihr euch wiederfandet im Krug,
langsam erkühlend und Warmes der Mädchen, wie
    Beichten,

von euch gebend, wie trübe ermüdende Sünden,
die das Gepflücktsein beging, als Bezug
wieder zu ihnen, die sich euch blühend verbünden.

# VII

Flowers, you who are kin to the hands that arrange
(gentle girls' hands of present and past),
who often lay on the garden table, from edge
to edge, exhausted and slightly bruised,

waiting for the water once more to bring you back whole
from the death that had just begun—and now
lifted again between the fast-streaming poles
of sensitive fingers that are able to do

even more good than you guessed, as you lightly uncurled,
coming to yourselves again in the pitcher,
slowly cooling, and exhaling the warmth of girls

like long confessions, like dreary wearying sins
committed by being plucked, which once more
relate you to those who in blossoming are your cousins.

## VIII

Wenige ihr, der einstigen Kindheit Gespielen
in den zerstreuten Gärten der Stadt:
wie wir uns fanden und uns zögernd gefielen
und, wie das Lamm mit dem redenden Blatt,

sprachen als Schweigende. Wenn wir uns einmal freuten,
keinem gehörte es. Wessen wars?
Und wie zergings unter allen den gehenden Leuten
und im Bangen des langen Jahrs.

Wagen umrollten uns fremd, vorübergezogen,
Häuser umstanden uns stark, aber unwahr,—und keines
kannte uns je. *Was* war wirklich im All?

Nichts. Nur die Bälle. Ihre herrlichen Bogen.
Auch nicht die Kinder . . . Aber manchmal trat eines,
ach ein vergehendes, unter den fallenden Ball.

*(In memoriam Egon von Rilke)*

# VIII

You playmates of mine in the scattered parks of the city,
small friends from a childhood of long ago:
how we found and liked one another, hesitantly,
and, like the lamb with the talking scroll,

spoke with our silence. When we were filled with joy,
it belonged to no one: it was simply there.
And how it dissolved among all the adults who passed by
and in the fears of the endless year.

Wheels rolled past us, we stood and stared at the carriages;
houses surrounded us, solid but untrue—and none
of them ever knew us. *What* in that world was real?

Nothing. Only the balls. Their magnificent arches.
Not even the children . . . But sometimes one,
oh a vanishing one, stepped under the plummeting ball.

*(In memoriam Egon von Rilke)*

## IX

Rühmt euch, ihr Richtenden, nicht der entbehrlichen Folter
und daß das Eisen nicht länger an Hälsen sperrt.
Keins ist gesteigert, kein Herz—, weil ein gewollter
Krampf der Milde euch zarter verzerrt.

Was es durch Zeiten bekam, das schenkt das Schafott
wieder zurück, wie Kinder ihr Spielzeug vom vorig
alten Geburtstag. Ins reine, ins hohe, ins thorig
offene Herz träte er anders, der Gott

wirklicher Milde. Er käme gewaltig und griffe
strahlender um sich, wie Göttliche sind.
*Mehr* als ein Wind für die großen gesicherten Schiffe.

Weniger nicht, als die heimliche leise Gewahrung,
die uns im Innern schweigend gewinnt
wie ein still spielendes Kind aus unendlicher Paarung.

## IX

Don't boast, you judges, that you have dispensed with
  torture
and that convicts are no longer shackled by the neck or heel.
No heart is enhanced, not one is—because a tender
spasm of mercy twists your mouths into a smile.

What the scaffold received through the ages, it has given
  back
again, as children give back their battered old
birthday toys. Into the pure and lofty and gatelike
open heart he would differently enter, the god

of true mercy. Sudden, huge, he would stride through and
  grip
us dazzled with radiance all around.
*More* than a wind for the massive confident ships.

And not any less transforming than the deep intuition
that wins us over without a sound
like a quietly playing child of an infinite union.

## X

Alles Erworbne bedroht die Maschine, solange
sie sich erdreistet, im Geist, statt im Gehorchen, zu sein.
Daß nicht der herrlichen Hand schöneres Zögern mehr
    prange,
zu dem entschlossenern Bau schneidet sie steifer den Stein.

Nirgends bleibt sie zurück, daß wir ihr *ein* Mal entrönnen
und sie in stiller Fabrik ölend sich selber gehört.
Sie ist das Leben,—sie meint es am besten zu können,
die mit dem gleichen Entschluß ordnet und schafft und
    zerstört.

Aber noch ist uns das Dasein verzaubert; an hundert
Stellen ist es noch Ursprung. Ein Spielen von reinen
Kräften, die keiner berührt, der nicht kniet und bewundert.

Worte gehen noch zart am Unsäglichen aus . . .
Und die Musik, immer neu, aus den bebendsten Steinen,
baut im unbrauchbaren Raum ihr vergöttlichtes Haus.

# X

All we have gained the machine threatens, as long
as it dares to exist in the mind and not in obedience.
To dim the masterful hand's more glorious lingering,
for the determined structure it more rigidly cuts the stones.

Nowhere does it stay behind; we cannot escape it at last
as it rules, self-guided, self-oiled, from its silent factory.
It thinks it is life: thinks it does everything best,
though with equal determination it can create or destroy.

But still, existence for us is a miracle; in a hundred
places it is still the source. A playing of absolute
forces that no one can touch who has not knelt down in
     wonder.

Still there are words that can calmly approach the unsayable . . .
And from the most tremulous stones music, forever new,
builds in unusable space her deified temple.

## XI

Manche, des Todes, entstand ruhig geordnete Regel,
weiterbezwingender Mensch, seit du im Jagen beharrst;
mehr doch als Falle und Netz, weiß ich dich, Streifen von
    Segel,
den man hinuntergehängt in den höhligen Karst.

Leise ließ man dich ein, als wärst du ein Zeichen,
Frieden zu feiern. Doch dann: rang dich am Rande der
    Knecht,
—und, aus den Höhlen, die Nacht warf eine Handvoll von
    bleichen
taumelnden Tauben ins Licht . . .
                                    Aber auch *das* ist im Recht.

Fern von dem Schauenden sei jeglicher Hauch des
    Bedauerns,
nicht nur vom Jäger allein, der, was sich zeitig erweist,
wachsam und handelnd vollzieht.

*Töten ist eine Gestalt unseres wandernden Trauerns* . . .
Rein ist im heiteren Geist,
was an uns selber geschieht.

## XI

Many calmly established rules of death have arisen,
ever-conquering man, since you acquired a taste
for hunting; yet more than all traps, I know you, sailcloths of
    linen
that used to be hung down into the caverns of Karst.

Gently they lowered you in as if you were a signal
to celebrate peace. But then: the boy began shaking your
    side,
—and suddenly, from the caves, the darkness would fling
    out a handful
of pale doves into the day . . .
                                    But even that is all right.

Let every last twinge of pity be far from those who look on—
far not just from the conscience of the vigilant, steadfast
    hunter
who fulfills what time has allowed.

*Killing too is a form of our ancient wandering affliction . . .*
When the mind stays serene, whatever
happens to us is good.

## XII

Wolle die Wandlung. O sei für die Flamme begeistert,
drin sich ein Ding dir entzieht, das mit Verwandlungen
    prunkt;
jener entwerfende Geist, welcher das Irdische meistert,
liebt in dem Schwung der Figur nichts wie den wendenden
    Punkt.

Was sich ins Bleiben verschließt, schon *ists* das Erstarrte;
wähnt es sich sicher im Schutz des unscheinbaren Grau's?
Warte, ein Härtestes warnt aus der Ferne das Harte.
Wehe—: abwesender Hammer holt aus!

Wer sich als Quelle ergießt, den erkennt die Erkennung;
und sie führt ihn entzückt durch das heiter Geschaffne,
das mit Anfang oft schließt und mit Ende beginnt.

Jeder glückliche Raum ist Kind oder Enkel von Trennung,
den sie staunend durchgehn. Und die verwandelte Daphne
will, seit sie lorbeern fühlt, daß du dich wandelst in Wind.

## XII

*Will* transformation. Oh be inspired for the flame
in which a Thing disappears and bursts into something else;
the spirit of re-creation which masters this earthly form
loves most the pivoting point where you are no longer
    yourself.

What tightens into survival is already inert;
how safe is it really in its inconspicuous gray?
From far off a far greater hardness warns what is hard,
and the absent hammer is lifted high!

He who pours himself out like a stream is acknowledged at
    last by Knowledge;
and she leads him enchanted through the harmonious
    country
that finishes often with starting, and with ending begins.

Every fortunate space that the two of them pass through,
    astonished,
is a child or grandchild of parting. And the transfigured
    Daphne,
as she feels herself become laurel, wants you to change into
    wind.

## XIII

Sei allem Abschied voran, als wäre er hinter
dir, wie der Winter, der eben geht.
Denn unter Wintern ist einer so endlos Winter,
daß, überwinternd, dein Herz überhaupt übersteht.

Sei immer tot in Eurydike—, singender steige,
preisender steige zurück in den reinen Bezug.
Hier, unter Schwindenden, sei, im Reiche der Neige,
sei ein klingendes Glas, das sich im Klang schon zerschlug.

Sei—und wisse zugleich des Nicht-Seins Bedingung,
den unendlichen Grund deiner innigen Schwingung,
daß du sie völlig vollziehst dieses einzige Mal.

Zu dem gebrauchten sowohl, wie zum dumpfen und
       stummen
Vorrat der vollen Natur, den unsäglichen Summen,
zähle dich jubelnd hinzu und vernichte die Zahl.

# XIII

Be ahead of all parting, as though it already were
behind you, like the winter that has just gone by.
For among these winters there is one so endlessly winter
that only by wintering through it will your heart survive.

Be forever dead in Eurydice—more gladly arise
into the seamless life proclaimed in your song.
Here, in the realm of decline, among momentary days,
be the crystal cup that shattered even as it rang.

Be—and yet know the great void where all things begin,
the infinite source of your own most intense vibration,
so that, this once, you may give it your perfect assent.

To all that is used-up, and to all the muffled and dumb
creatures in the world's full reserve, the unsayable sums,
joyfully add your*self*, and cancel the count.

## XIV

Siehe die Blumen, diese dem Irdischen treuen,
denen wir Schicksal vom Rande des Schicksals leihn,—
aber wer weiß es! Wenn sie ihr Welken bereuen,
ist es an uns, ihre Reue zu sein.

Alles will schweben. Da gehn wir umher wie Beschwerer,
legen auf alles uns selbst, vom Gewichte entzückt;
o was sind wir den Dingen für zehrende Lehrer,
weil ihnen ewige Kindheit glückt.

Nähme sie einer ins innige Schlafen und schliefe
tief mit den Dingen—: o wie käme er leicht,
anders zum anderen Tag, aus der gemeinsamen Tiefe.

Oder er bliebe vielleicht; und sie blühten und priesen
ihn, den Bekehrten, der nun den Ihrigen gleicht,
allen den stillen Geschwistern im Winde der Wiesen.

## XIV

Look at the flowers, so faithful to what is earthly,
to whom we lend fate from the very border of fate.
And if they are sad about how they must wither and die,
perhaps it is our vocation to be their regret.

All Things want to fly. Only *we* are weighed down by desire,
caught in ourselves and enthralled with our heaviness.
Oh what consuming, negative teachers we are
for them, while eternal childhood fills them with grace.

If someone were to fall into intimate slumber, and slept
deeply with Things—: how easily he would come
to a different day, out of the mutual depth.

Or perhaps he would stay there; and they would blossom
        and praise
their newest convert, who now is like one of them,
all those silent companions in the wind of the meadows.

## XV

O Brunnen-Mund, du gebender, du Mund,
der unerschöpflich Eines, Reines, spricht,—
du, vor des Wassers fließendem Gesicht,
marmorne Maske. Und im Hintergrund

der Aquädukte Herkunft. Weither an
Gräbern vorbei, vom Hang des Apennins
tragen sie dir dein Sagen zu, das dann
am schwarzen Altern deines Kinns

vorüberfallt in das Gefäß davor.
Dies ist das schlafend hingelegte Ohr,
das Marmorohr, in das du immer sprichst.

Ein Ohr der Erde. Nur mit sich allein
redet sie also. Schiebt ein Krug sich ein,
so scheint es ihr, daß du sie unterbrichst.

## XV

O fountain-mouth, you generous, always-filled
mouth that speaks pure oneness, constantly—
you marble mask before the water's still
flowing face. And in the background, the

slow descent of aqueducts. From far
graves, and from the sloping Apennines,
they bring you all your syllables, which pour
down from your blackened, aging chin

into the basin lying underneath.
This is the intimate and sleeping ear,
the marble ear, in which you always speak.

An ear of Earth. Just with herself alone
does she talk this way. And if a jug slips in,
she feels that you are interrupting her.

## XVI

Immer wieder von uns aufgerissen,
ist der Gott die Stelle, welche heilt.
Wir sind Scharfe, denn wir wollen wissen,
aber er ist heiter und verteilt.

Selbst die reine, die geweihte Spende
nimmt er anders nicht in seine Welt,
als indem er sich dem freien Ende
unbewegt entgegenstellt.

Nur der Tote trinkt
aus der hier vons uns *gehörten* Quelle,
wenn der Gott ihm schweigend winkt, dem Toten.

*Uns* wird nur das Lärmen angeboten.
Und das Lamm erbittet seine Schelle
aus dem stilleren Instinkt.

# XVI

Over and over by us torn in two,
the god is the hidden place that heals again.
We are sharp-edged, because we want to know,
but he is always scattered and serene.

Even the pure, the consecrated gift
he takes into his world no other way
than by positioning himself, unmoved,
to face the one end that is free.

Only the dead may drink
from the source that we just hear, the unseen pool,
when the god, mute, allows them with a gesture.

Here, to us, only the noise is offered.
And the lamb keeps begging for its bell
because of a more quiet instinct.

## XVII

Wo, in welchen immer selig bewässerten Gärten, an welchen
Bäumen, aus welchen zärtlich entblätterten Blüten-Kelchen
reifen die fremdartigen Früchte der Tröstung? Diese
köstlichen, deren du eine vielleicht in der zertretenen Wiese

deiner Armut findest. Von einem zum anderen Male
wunderst du dich über die Größe der Frucht,
über ihr Heilsein, über die Sanftheit der Schale,
und daß sie der Leichtsinn des Vogels dir nicht vorwegnahm
    und nicht die Eifersucht

unten des Wurms. Giebt es denn Bäume, von Engeln
    beflogen,
und von verborgenen langsamen Gärtnern so seltsam
    gezogen,
daß sie uns tragen, ohne uns zu gehören?

Haben wir niemals vermocht, wir Schatten und Schemen,
durch unser voreilig reifes und wieder welkes Benehmen
jener gelassenen Sommer Gleichmut zu stören?

## XVII

Where, inside what forever blissfully watered gardens, upon
    what trees,
out of what deep and tenderly unpetaled flower-cups,
do the exotic fruits of consolation hang ripening? Those
rare delicacies, of which you find one perhaps

in the trampled meadows of your poverty. Time and again
you have stood there marveling over the sheer size of the
    fruit,
over its wholeness, its smooth and unmottled skin,
and that the lightheaded bird or the jealous worm under the
    ground had not

snatched it away from your hands. *Are* there such trees,
    flown through
by angels and so strangely cared for by gardeners hidden and
    slow
that they bear their fruit to nourish us, without being ours?

Is it true we have never been able (we who are only
shadows and shades), through our ripening and wilting so
    early,
to disturb the enormous calm of those patient summers?

## XVIII

Tänzerin: o du Verlegung
alles Vergehens in Gang: wie brachtest du's dar.
Und der Wirbel am Schluß, dieser Baum aus Bewegung,
nahm er nicht ganz in Besitz das erschwungene Jahr?

Blühte nicht, daß ihn dein Schwingen von vorhin
    umschwärme,
plötzlich sein Wipfel von Stille? Und über ihr,
war sie nicht Sonne, war sie nicht Sommer, die Wärme,
diese unzählige Wärme aus dir?

Aber er trug auch, er trug, dein Baum der Ekstase.
Sind sie nicht seine ruhigen Früchte: der Krug,
reifend gestreift, und die gereiftere Vase?

Und in den Bildern: ist nicht die Zeichnung geblieben,
die deiner Braue dunkler Zug
rasch an die Wandung der eigenen Wendung geschrieben?

## XVIII

Dancing girl: transformation
of all transience into steps: how you offered it there.
And the arm-raised whirl at the end, that tree made of
    motion,
didn't it fully possess the pivoted year?

Didn't it, so that your previous swirling might swarm
in the midst of it, suddenly blossom with stillness? And
    above,
wasn't it sunshine, wasn't it summer, the warmth,
the pure, immeasurable warmth that you gave?

But it bore fruit also, it bore fruit, your tree of bliss.
Aren't they here in their tranquil season: the jug,
whirling to ripeness, and the even more ripened vase?

And in the pictures: can't we still see the drawing
which your eyebrow's dark evanescent stroke
quickly inscribed on the surface of its own turning?

## XIX

Irgendwo wohnt das Gold in der verwöhnenden Bank
und mit Tausenden tut es vertraulich. Doch jener
Blinde, der Bettler, ist selbst dem kupfernen Zehner
wie ein verlorener Ort, wie das staubige Eck unterm
    Schrank.

In den Geschäften entlang ist das Geld wie zuhause
und verkleidet sich scheinbar in Seide, Nelken und Pelz.
Er, der Schweigende, steht in der Atempause
alles des wach oder schlafend atmenden Gelds.

O wie mag sie sich schließen bei Nacht, diese immer offene
    Hand.
Morgen holt sie das Schicksal wieder, und täglich
hält es sie hin: hell, elend, unendlich zerstörbar.

Daß doch einer, ein Schauender, endlich ihren langen
    Bestand
staunend begriffe und rühmte. Nur dem Aufsingenden
    säglich.
Nur dem Göttlichen hörbar.

## XIX

Somewhere gold lives, luxurious, inside the pampering bank,
on intimate terms with thousands. Meanwhile, the wretched
blindman begging here seems, even to a penny, just like
some always-forgotten corner or the dustpile beneath a bed.

In all the most elegant shops money is at ease
and steps out in shiny costumes of furs, carnations, and silks.
He, the silent one, stands in the narrow breath-pause
made by money breathing as it slumbers or wakes.

Oh how can it close at night, that hand which is always
    open?
Tomorrow and each day Fate will arrive and hold it out:
    clear,
squalid, at any moment likely to be destroyed.

If only someone who could *see,* astonished at its long
    duration,
would understand it and praise it. Sayable only for the
    singer.
Audible only to the god.

## XX

Zwischen den Sternen, wie weit; und doch, um wievieles
    noch weiter,
was man am Hiesigen lernt.
Einer, zum Beispiel, ein Kind . . . und ein Nächster, ein
    Zweiter—,
o wie unfaßlich entfernt.

Schicksal, es mißt uns vielleicht mit des Seienden Spanne,
daß es uns fremd erscheint;
denk, wieviel Spannen allein vom Mädchen zum Manne,
wenn es ihn meidet und meint.

Alles ist weit—, und nirgends schließt sich der Kreis.
Sieh in der Schüssel, auf heiter bereitetem Tische,
seltsam der Fische Gesicht.

Fische sind stumm . . . , meinte man einmal. Wer weiß?
Aber ist nicht am Ende ein Ort, wo man das, was der Fische
Sprache wäre, *ohne* sie spricht?

## XX

In between stars, what distances; and yet, how much vaster
    the distance
that we learn from what is right *here*.
Someone, for example a child . . . and beside him, his brother
    or sister—
oh how incomprehensibly far.

Fate measures us perhaps according to what is real,
so it seems to us not our own;
think of how vast a distance there is from the girl
to the loved and avoided man.

All things are far—and nowhere does the circle close.
Look at the fish, served up on the gaily set table:
how peculiar its face on the dish.

All fish are mute . . . , one used to think. But who knows?
Isn't there at last a place where, *without* them, we would be
    able
to speak in the language of fish?

## XXI

Singe die Gärten, mein Herz, die du nicht kennst; wie in
    Glas
eingegossene Gärten, klar, unerreichbar.
Wasser und Rosen von Ispahan oder Schiras,
singe sie selig, preise sie, keinem vergleichbar.

Zeige, mein Herz, daß du sie niemals entbehrst.
Daß sie dich meinen, ihre reifenden Feigen.
Daß du mit ihren, zwischen den blühenden Zweigen
wie zum Gesicht gesteigerten Lüften verkehrst.

Meide den Irrtum, daß es Entbehrungen gebe
für den geschehnen Entschluß, diesen: zu sein!
Seidener Faden, kamst du hinein ins Gewebe.

Welchem der Bilder du auch im Innern geeint bist
(sei es selbst ein Moment aus dem Leben der Pein),
fühl, daß der ganze, der rühmliche Teppich gemeint ist.

# XXI

Sing of the gardens, my heart, that you never saw; as if glass
domes had been placed upon them, unreached forever.
Fountains and roses of Ispahan or Shiraz—
sing of their happiness, praise them: unlike all others.

Show that you always feel them, forever close.
That when their figs ripen, it is you they are ripening for.
That you know every breeze which, among the blossoms
     they bear,
is intensified till it almost becomes a face.

Avoid the illusion that there can be any lack
for someone who wishes, then fully decides: to be!
Silken thread, you were woven into the fabric.

Whatever the design with which you are inwardly joined
(even for only one moment amid years of grief),
feel that the whole, the marvelous carpet is meant.

## XXII

O trotz Schicksal: die herrlichen Überflüsse
unseres Daseins, in Parken übergeschäumt,—
oder als steinerne Männer neben die Schlüsse
hoher Portale, unter Balkone gebäumt!

O die eherne Glocke, die ihre Keule
täglich wider den stumpfen Alltag hebt.
Oder die *eine*, in Karnak, die Säule, die Säule,
die fast ewige Tempel überlebt.

Heute stürzen die Überschüsse, dieselben,
nur noch als Eile vorbei, aus dem waagrechten gelben
Tag in die blendend mit Licht übertriebene Nacht.

Aber das Rasen zergeht und läßt keine Spuren.
Kurven des Flugs durch die Luft und die, die sie fuhren,
keine vielleicht ist umsonst. Doch nur wie gedacht.

# XXII

Oh in spite of fate: the glorious overflowings
of our existence, spouted upward in parks—
or as stone-carved men who bear upon shoulders and backs
the weight overhead, braced on the sheer edge of buildings.

Oh the bronze bell that, day after day, can lift
its club to shatter our dull quotidian hum.
Or the *only* presence, in Karnak, the column, the column
in which temples that were almost eternal have been
    outlived.

For us these abundances plunge past, no longer central
but only appearing as haste, out of the horizontal
yellow day and into the overwhelmed, dazzled night.

But this frenzy too will subside, leaving no traces.
Arcs of airplanes and those who drove them through space,
none perhaps is in vain. Yet only as thought.

## XXIII

Rufe mich zu jener deiner Stunden,
die dir unaufhörlich widersteht:
flehend nah wie das Gesicht von Hunden,
aber immer wieder weggedreht,

wenn du meinst, sie endlich zu erfassen.
So Entzognes ist am meisten dein.
Wir sind frei. Wir wurden dort entlassen,
wo wir meinten, erst begrüßt zu sein.

Bang verlangen wir nach einem Halte,
wir zu Jungen manchmal für das Alte
und zu alt für das, was niemals war.

Wir, gerecht nur, wo wir dennoch preisen,
weil wir, ach, der Ast sind und das Eisen
und das Süße reifender Gefahr.

# XXIII

Call me to the one among your moments
that stands against you, ineluctably:
intimate as a dog's imploring glance
but, again, forever, turned away

when you think you've captured it at last.
What seems so far from you is most your own.
We are already free, and were dismissed
where we thought we soon would be at home.

Anxious, we keep longing for a foothold—
we, at times too young for what is old
and too old for what has never been;

doing justice only where we praise,
because we are the branch, the iron blade,
and sweet danger, ripening from within.

## XXIV

O diese Lust, immer neu, aus gelockertem Lehm!
Niemand beinah hat den frühesten Wagern geholfen.
Städte entstanden trotzdem an beseligten Golfen,
Wasser und Öl füllten die Krüge trotzdem.

Götter, wir planen sie erst in erkühnten Entwürfen,
die uns das mürrische Schicksal wieder zerstört.
Aber sie sind die Unsterblichen. Sehet, wir dürfen
jenen erhorchen, der uns am Ende erhört.

Wir, ein Geschlecht durch Jahrtausende: Mütter und Väter,
immer erfüllter von dem künftigen Kind,
daß es uns einst, übersteigend, erschüttere, später.

Wir, wir unendlich Gewagten, was haben wir Zeit!
Und nur der schweigsame Tod, der weiß, was wir sind
und was er immer gewinnt, wenn er uns leiht.

## XXIV

Oh the delight, ever new, out of loosened soil!
The ones who first dared were almost without any help.
Nonetheless, at fortunate harbors, cities sprang up,
and pitchers were nonetheless filled with water and oil.

Gods: we project them first in the boldest of sketches,
which sullen Fate keeps crumpling and tossing away.
But for all that, the gods are immortal. Surely we may
hear out the one who, in the end, will hear *us*.

We, one generation through thousands of lifetimes: women
and men, who are more and more filled with the child we
        will bear,
so that through it we may be shattered and overtaken.

We, the endlessly dared—how far we have come!
And only taciturn Death can know what we are
and how he must always profit when he lends us time.

## XXV

Schon, horch, hörst du der ersten Harken
Arbeit; wieder den menschlichen Takt
in der verhaltenen Stille der starken
Vorfrühlingserde. Unabgeschmackt

scheint dir das Kommende. Jenes so oft
dir schon Gekommene scheint dir zu kommen
wieder wie Neues. Immer erhofft,
nahmst du es niemals. Es hat dich genommen.

Selbst die Blätter durchwinterter Eichen
scheinen im Abend ein künftiges Braun.
Manchmal geben sich Lüfte ein Zeichen.

Schwarz sind die Sträucher. Doch Haufen von Dünger
lagern als satteres Schwarz in den Aun.
Jede Stunde, die hingeht, wird jünger.

## XXV

Already (listen!) you can hear the first
harrows; once more the rhythm of men
through the held-back silence of the resolute earth
in early spring. What has so often

come to you is coming once more,
vivid as if for the first time. Now,
slowly, you await what you always hoped for
but never took. It always took *you*.

Even the leaves of wintered-through oaks
seem in the twilight a future brown.
Breezes signal, then signal back.

Black are the bushes. Yet heaps of dung
lie more intensely black on the ground.
Every hour that goes by grows younger.

## XXVI

Wie ergreift uns der Vogelschrei . . .
Irgend ein einmal erschaffenes Schreien.
Aber die Kinder schon, spielend im Freien,
schreien an wirklichen Schreien vorbei.

Schreien den Zufall. In Zwischenräume
dieses, des Weltraums, (in welchen der heile
Vogelschrei eingeht, wie Menschen in Träume—)
treiben sie ihre, des Kreischens, Keile.

Wehe, wo sind wir? Immer noch freier,
wie die losgerissenen Drachen
jagen wir halbhoch, mit Rändern von Lachen,

windig zerfetzten.—Ordne die Schreier,
singender Gott! daß sie rauschend erwachen,
tragend als Strömung das Haupt und die Leier.

## XXVI

How deeply the cry of a bird can move us . . .
*Any* cry that is cried out whole.
But children, playing in their open space—
already their cries have become unreal.

They cry out chance. And into the silent
seamless world, into which birds' cries
fully (as men into dream-space) blend,
they hammer the hard-edged wedge of their noise.

Alas, where are we? Freer and freer,
like colored kites torn loose from their strings,
we toss half-high-up, framed by cold laughter,

slashed by the wind.—Oh compose the criers,
harmonious god! let them wake resounding,
let their clear stream carry the head and the lyre.

## XXVII

Giebt es wirklich die Zeit, die zerstörende?
Wann, auf dem ruhenden Berg, zerbricht sie die Burg?
Dieses Herz, das unendlich den Göttern gehörende,
wann vergewaltigts der Demiurg?

Sind wir wirklich so ängstlich Zerbrechliche,
wie das Schicksal uns wahr machen will?
Ist die Kindheit, die tiefe, versprechliche,
in den Wurzeln—später—still?

Ach, das Gespenst des Vergänglichen,
durch den arglos Empfänglichen
geht es, als wär es ein Rauch.

Als die, die wir sind, als die Treibenden,
gelten wir doch bei bleibenden
Kräften als göttlicher Brauch.

# XXVII

Does it really exist, Time, the Destroyer?
When will it crush the fortress on the peaceful height?
This heart, which belongs to the infinite gods forever,
when will the Demiurge violate it?

Are we really as fate keeps trying to convince us,
weak and brittle in an alien world?
And childhood, with all its divining voices,
is it later, down to its first root, stilled?

Ah, the ghost of the transient
moves through the open, innocent
heart like a summer cloud.

As who we are, desperate, driving,
we still matter among the abiding
powers as a use of the gods.

## XXVIII

O komm und geh. Du, fast noch Kind, ergänze
für einen Augenblick die Tanzfigur
zum reinen Sternbild einer jener Tänze,
darin wir die dumpf ordnende Natur

vergänglich übertreffen. Denn sie regte
sich völlig hörend nur, da Orpheus sang.
Du warst noch die von damals her Bewegte
und leicht befremdet, wenn ein Baum sich lang

besann, mit dir nach dem Gehör zu gehn.
Du wußtest noch die Stelle, wo die Leier
sich tönend hob—; die unerhörte Mitte.

Für sie versuchtest du die schönen Schritte
und hofftest, einmal zu der heilen Feier
des Freundes Gang und Antlitz hinzudrehn.

# XXVIII

Oh come and go. You, almost still a child—
for just a moment fill out the dance-figure
into the constellation of those bold
dances in which dull, obsessive Nature

is fleetingly surpassed. For she was stirred
to total hearing just when Orpheus sang.
You were still moved by those primeval words
and a bit surprised if any tree took long

to step with you into the listening ear.
You knew the place where once the lyre arose
resounding: the unheard, unheard-of center.

For *its* sake you tried out your lovely motion
and hoped that you would one day turn your friend's
body toward the perfect celebration.

## XXIX

Stiller Freund der vielen Fernen, fühle,
wie dein Atem noch den Raum vermehrt.
Im Gebälk der finstern Glockenstühle
laß dich läuten. Das, was an dir zehrt,

wird ein Starkes über dieser Nahrung.
Geh in der Verwandlung aus und ein.
Was ist deine leidendste Erfahrung?
Ist dir Trinken bitter, werde Wein.

Sei in dieser Nacht aus Übermaß
Zauberkraft am Kreuzweg deiner Sinne,
ihrer seltsamen Begegnung Sinn.

Und wenn dich das Irdische vergaß,
zu der stillen Erde sag: Ich rinne.
Zu dem raschen Wasser sprich: Ich bin.

## XXIX

Silent friend of many distances, feel
how your breath enlarges all of space.
Let your presence ring out like a bell
into the night. What feeds upon your face

grows mighty from the nourishment thus offered.
Move through transformation, out and in.
What is the deepest loss that you have suffered?
If drinking is bitter, change yourself to wine.

In this immeasurable darkness, be the power
that rounds your senses in their magic ring,
the sense of their mysterious encounter.

And if the earthly no longer knows your name,
whisper to the silent earth: I'm flowing.
To the flashing water say: I am.

# *Appendix to The Sonnets to Orpheus*

## [I]

Rühmen, das ists! Ein zum Rühmen Bestellter,
ging er hervor wie das Erz aus des Steins
Schweigen. Sein Herz, o vergängliche Kelter
eines den Menschen unendlichen Weins!

Euch kanns beirren, wenn man in Grüften
Könige aufdeckt, verfault und verwürmt,—
ihn hat der Hinfall der Häupter und Hüften
zwar mit zehrendem Weh bestürmt,

aber der Zweifel war ihm verächtlich.
Er zerrang den Gestank und pries
Tägiges täglich und Nächtiges nächtlich,

denn wer erkennt die verwandelten Gnaden?
Knieend aus dem Markte der Maden
hob er das heile Goldene Vließ.

# [I]

Praising is what matters! He was summoned for that,
and came to us like the ore from a stone's
silence. His mortal heart presses out
a deathless, inexhaustible wine!

Don't be confused if kings are discovered
rotting in their sepulchers, gnawed by the worm—
for a while the decay of body and head
assailed him too with intense alarm;

he, however, despising all doubt,
throttled the stench and with praise affirmed
the daily by day and the nightly at night,

for who knows what is transformed by the graces?
Kneeling from the maggots' marketplace,
he lifted the Golden Fleece, unharmed.

## [II]

O das Neue, Freunde, ist nicht dies,
daß Maschinen uns die Hand verdrängen.
Laßt euch nicht beirrn von Übergängen,
bald wird schweigen, wer das 'Neue' pries.

Denn das Ganze ist unendlich neuer,
als ein Kabel und ein hohes Haus.
Seht, die Sterne sind ein altes Feuer,
und die neuern Feuer löschen aus.

Glaubt nicht, daß die längsten Transmissionen
schon des Künftigen Räder drehn.
Denn Aeonen reden mit Aeonen.

Mehr, als wir erfuhren, ist geschehn.
Und die Zukunft faßt das Allerfernste
rein in eins mit unserm innern Ernste.

[II]

The New, my friends, is not a matter of
letting machines force out our handiwork.
Don't be confused by change; soon those who have
praised the "New" will realize their mistake.

For look, the Whole is infinitely newer
than a cable or a high apartment house.
The stars keep blazing with an ancient fire,
and all more recent fires will fade out.

Not even the longest, strongest of transmissions
can turn the wheels of what will be.
Across the moment, aeons speak with aeons.

*More* than we experienced has gone by.
And the future holds the most remote event
in union with what we most deeply want.

[III]

Brau uns den Zauber, in dem die Grenzen sich lösen,
immer zum Feuer gebeugter Geist!
Diese, vor allem, heimliche Grenze des Bösen,
die auch den Ruhenden, der sich nicht rührte, umkreist.

Löse mit einigen Tropfen das Engende jener
Grenze der Zeiten, die uns belügt;
denn wie tief ist in uns noch der Tag der Athener
und der ägyptische Gott oder Vogel gefügt.

Ruhe nicht eher, bis auch der Rand der Geschlechter,
der sich sinnlos verringenden, schmolz.
Öffne die Kindheit und die Schooße gerechter

gebender Mütter, daß sie, Beschämer der Leere,
unbeirrt durch das hindernde Holz
künftige Ströme gebären, Vermehrer der Meere.

[III]

Brew us the magic in which all limits dissolve,
spirit forever bent to the fire!
That fathomless limit of evil, first, which revolves
also around those who are resting and do not stir.

Dissolve with a few drops whatever excludes in the limit
of the ages, which makes our past wisdom a fraud;
for how deeply we have absorbed the Athenian sunlight
and the mystery of the Egyptian falcon or god.

Don't rest until the boundary that keeps the sexes
in meaningless conflict has disappeared.
Open up childhood and the wombs of more truly expectant

generous mothers so that, shaming all that is empty,
and not confused by the hindering wood,
they may give birth to future rivers, augmenting the sea.

[IV]

Mehr nicht sollst du wissen als die Stele
und im reinen Stein das milde Bild:
beinah heiter, nur so leicht als fehle
ihr die Mühe, die auf Erden gilt.

Mehr nicht sollst du fühlen als die reine
Richtung im unendlichen Entzug—
ach, vielleicht das Kaltsein jener Steine,
die sie manchmal abends trug.

Aber sonst sei dir die Tröstung teuer,
die du im Gewohntesten erkennst.
Wind ist Trost, und Tröstung ist das Feuer.

Hier- und Dortsein, dich ergreife beides
seltsam ohne Unterschied. Du trennst
sonst das Weißsein von dem Weiß des Kleides.

[IV]

Seek no more than what the stela knows,
and the mild image sculpted in the stone:
almost cheerfully, with a lightness, as
though they were exempt from earthly pain.

Experience no further than the pure
direction in the world's withdrawing stream—
ah, perhaps the icy jewels she wore
in that dimly lighted room.

Be all the more consoled by what you see in
the elements that are most truly yours.
Wind consoles, and fire is consolation.

Here and There: you must be gripped by both,
strangely without a difference. Otherwise
you drain the whiteness from the whitest cloth.

## [V]

Denk: Sie hätten vielleicht aneinander erfahren,
welches die teilbaren Wunder sind—.
Doch da er sich langsam verrang an den alternden Jahren,
war sie die Künftige erst, ein kommendes Kind.

*Sie*, vielleicht—, *sie*, die da ging und mit Freundinnen
  spielte,
hat er im knabigen schon, im Erahnen, ersehnt,
wissend das schließende Herz, das ihn völlig enthielte,
und nun trennt sie ein Nichts, ein verfünftes Jahrzehnt.

Oh du ratloser Gott, du betrogener Hymen,
wie du die Fackel nach abwärts kehrst,
weil sie ihm Asche warf an die grauende Schläfe.

Soll er klagend vergehn und die Beginnende rühmen?
Oder sein stillster Verzicht, wird er sie erst
machen zu jener Gestalt, die ihn ganz überträfe?

[V]

Imagine: they might have experienced through each other
which of our miracles can be shared—.
But while he gradually wrestled with growing older,
she was as yet unborn, a still-future child.

*She*, perhaps—still playing with her friends, it was *she*
whom he had foreseen with boyish longing and love,
knowing the heart that would one day hold him completely;
and now a mere nothing parts them: a decade times five.

Oh you bewildered god, you defrauded Hymen,
how sadly you extinguish the wedding-torch now
because it flung ashes onto that graying head.

Must he die in laments, and praise the beginning woman?
Or through his most silent yielding will he make her into
that unmoving form by which he is wholly exceeded?

## [VI]

Aber, ihr Freunde, zum Fest, laßt uns gedenken der Feste,
wenn uns ein eigenes nicht, mitten im Umzug, gelingt.
Seht, sie meinen auch uns, alle der Villa d'Este
spielende Brunnen, wenn auch nicht mehr ein jeglicher
    springt.

Wir sind die Erben, trotzdem, dieser gesungenen Gärten;
Freunde, o faßt sie im Ernst, diese besitzende Pflicht.
Was uns als Letzten vielleicht glückliche Götter gewährten,
hat keinen ehrlichen Platz im zerstreuten Verzicht.

Keiner der Götter vergeh. Wir brauchen sie alle und jeden,
jedes gelte uns noch, jedes gestaltete Bild.
Laßt euch, was ruhig geruht, nicht in den Herzen zerreden.

Sind wir auch anders, als die, denen noch Feste gelangen,
dieser leistende Strahl, der uns als Stärke entquillt,
ist über große, zu uns, Aquädukte gegangen.

[VI]

When everything we create is far in spirit from the festive,
in the midst of our turbulent days let us think of what
	festivals *were*.
Look, they still play for us also, all of the Villa d'Este's
glittering fountains, though some are no longer towering
	there.

Still, we are heirs to those gardens that poets once praised in
	their songs;
let us grasp our most urgent duty: to make them fully our
	own.
We perhaps are the last to be given such god-favored,
	fortunate Things,
their final chance to find an enduring home.

Let not one god pass away. We all need each of them now,
let each be valid for us, each image formed in the depths.
Don't speak with the slightest disdain of whatever the heart
	can know.

Though we are no longer the ones for whom great festivals
	thrived,
this accomplishing fountain-jet that surges to us as strength
has traveled through aqueducts—in order, for our sake, to
	arrive.

## [VII]

Welche Stille um einen Gott! Wie hörst du in ihr
jeden Wechsel im Auffall des Brunnenstrahls
am weilenden Wasser des Marmorovals.
Und am Lorbeer vorüber ein Fühlen: drei oder vier

Blätter, die ein Falter gestreift hat. An dir
taumelt er hin, im tragenden Atem des Tals.
Und du gedenkst eines anderen Mals,
da sie dir schon so vollkommen schien, hier,

diese Stille um einen Gott. Ward sie nicht *mehr*?
Nimmt sie nicht zu? Nimmt sie nicht überhand?
Drängt sie nicht fast wie ein Widerstand

an dein tönendes Herz? Irgendwo bricht sich sein Schlag
an einer lautlosen Pause im Tag . . .
Dort ist Er.

## [VII]

What silence around a god! How, inside it, you hear
every change in the sparkling fountain-spray
on the marble pool, as it leaps up and falls back entirely.
And over the laurel a feeling: three, perhaps four

leaves that a butterfly touched. With a whir
it goes tumbling past, on the buoyant breath of the valley.
And now you remember another day
when you felt it, already so perfect, here,

the silence around a god. But was it like this?
Isn't it spreading? Isn't it immense?
Isn't it pressing almost like a resistance

upon your resounding heart? Somewhere its beat is broken
on a soundless lull in the afternoon . . .
There, He is.

[VIII]

Wir hören seit lange die Brunnen mit.
Sie klingen uns beinah wie Zeit.
Aber sie halten viel eher Schritt
mit der wandelnden Ewigkeit.

Das Wasser ist fremd und das Wasser ist dein,
von hier und *doch* nicht von hier.
Eine Weile bist du der Brunnenstein,
und es spiegelt die Dinge in dir.

Wie ist das alles entfernt und verwandt
und lange enträtselt und unerkannt,
sinnlos und wieder voll Sinn.

Dein ist, zu lieben, was du nicht weißt.
Es nimmt dein geschenktes Gefühl und reißt
es mit sich hinüber. Wohin?

[VIII]

We have overheard fountains all our days.
They sound to us almost like time.
But much more closely do they keep pace
with eternity's subtle rhythm.

The water is strange and the water is yours,
from here and from far below.
You are the fountain-stone, unawares,
and all Things are mirrored in you.

How distant this is, yet deeply akin,
long unriddled and never known,
senseless, then perfectly clear.

Your task is to love what you don't understand.
It grips your most secret emotion, and
rushes away with it. Where?

[IX]

Wann war ein Mensch je so wach
wie der Morgen von heut?
Nicht nur Blume und Bach,
auch das Dach ist erfreut.

Selbst sein alternder Rand,
von den Himmeln erhellt,—
wird fühlend: ist Land,
ist Antwort, ist Welt.

Alles atmet und dankt.
O ihr Nöte der Nacht,
wie ihr spurlos versankt.

Aus Scharen von Licht
war ihr Dunkel gemacht,
das sich rein widerspricht.

## [IX]

When was a *man* as awake
as this morning is?
Not just flower and brook:
the roof too rejoices.

Even its weathered rim,
lit by the sky—
finds it can feel: is home,
is answer, is day.

Everything breathes in accord.
How tracelessly you have gone
away, you cares of the night.

Its darkness was formed,
in pure contradiction,
from legions of light.

# [BRUCHSTÜCKE]

## [i]

So wie angehaltner Atem steht
steht die Nymphe in dem vollen Baume

## [ii]

Sieh hinauf. Heut ist der Nachtraum heiter.

## [iii]

Hoher Gott der fernen Vorgesänge
überall erfahr ich dich zutiefst
in der freien Ordnung mancher Hänge
stehn die Sträucher noch wie du sie riefst

## [iv]

Spiegel, du Doppelgänger des Raums! O Spiegel, in dich fort
stürzt die Hälfte der Lächeln / vielleicht die süßesten; denn
    wie
oft dem Meister der Strich, der probende, auf dem
vorläufigen Blatt blumiger aufschwingt, als später
auf dem bereiteten Grund der geführtere Umriß:
So, oh, lächelst du hin, Unsägliche, deiner
Morgen Herkunft und Freiheit in die immer
nehmenden Spiegel

## [v]

Immer, o Nymphe, seit je / hab ich dich staunend
    bewundert
ob du auch nie aus dem Baum mir dem verschlossenen
    tratst—.
Ich bin die Zeit die vergeht—, du bist ein junges
    Jahrhundert,
alles ist immer noch neu, was du von Göttern erbatst.

## [FRAGMENTS]

### [i]

Like held-in breath, serene and motionless
stands the nymph inside the ripening tree

### [ii]

Look up. How calm the heavens are tonight.

### [iii]

Lofty god of distant harmonies
I sense you everywhere deep in every Thing
upon the gently patterned slope the trees
stand silent as when first they heard you sing

### [iv]

Mirror, you doppelgänger of space! O mirror, into you go
plunging the halves of smiles / perhaps the sweetest; for how
often the master's preliminary brushstroke, upon the
provisional page more fruitfully leaps up than, later,
the more controlled outline does on the ready background:
So do you, O unsayable presence, smile forth
your morning's descent and freedom into the ever-
accepting mirrors

### [v]

Forever, O nymph, how long / I have marveled at you,
    amazed,
though you never stepped into my sight from out of the
    closed-in tree—.
I am the time that is passing—you are the youngest age,
all that you asked from the gods has remained here, forever
    new.

Dein ist die Wiese, sie schwankt noch jetzt von dem
    Sprunge,
jenem mit dem du zuletzt in die Ulme verschwandst.
Einst in der christlichen Früh. Und ist nicht, du junge,
*Dir* unser erstes Gefühl in den Frühling gepflanzt.

Eh uns ein Mädchen noch rührt, bist du die gemeinte

[vi]

. . . . . . . . . . Braun's

. . . . . . . . . an den sonoren
trockenen Boden des Walds
               trommelt das Flüchten des Fauns

[vii]

Dies ist das schweigende Steigen der Phallen

[viii]

Von meiner Antwort weiß ich noch nicht
wann ich sie sagen werde.
Aber, horch eine Harke, die schon schafft.
Oben allein im Weinberg spricht
schon ein Mann mit der Erde.

[ix]

Hast du des Epheus wechselnde Blättergestalten

[x]

Wahre dich besser
         wahre dich Wandrer
mit dem selber auch gehenden Weg

Yours is the meadow, even now it sways from the leap
with which you finally vanished into the elm.
Once, in the christian dawn. And our earliest hope:
for *your* sake isn't it planted into the springtime?

Before we are moved by a girl, it is you that we think
    of

[vi]

. . . . . . . . . . of the brown

. . . . . . . . . . on the sonorous
dried-up earth of the forest
            drums the flight of the faun

[vii]

This is the silent rising of the phalli

[viii]

About my answer: I still don't know
when I will bring it forth.
But listen, a harrow that already creates.
Up there in the vineyard someone, alone,
already speaks with the earth.

[ix]

Have you [?ever observed] the changing leaf-forms of
    the ivy

[x]

Protect yourself better
        protect yourself wanderer
with the road that is walking too

[xi]

Laß uns Legenden der Liebe hören.
Zeig uns ihr kühnes köstliches Leid.
Wo sie im Recht war, war alles Beschwören,
hier ist das meiste verleugneter Eid.

[xi]

Gather us now to hear love's legends.
Tell us of its daring, exquisite throes.
Where it was right, all things could be summoned;
here there are mostly abandoned vows.

# Notes

Notes

# Notes

## DUINO ELEGIES (1923)

The Elegies take their name from Duino Castle, on the Adriatic Sea, where Rilke spent the winter of 1911/1912 as a guest of his friend Princess Marie von Thurn und Taxis-Hohenlohe (1855–1934); they are dedicated to her in gratitude, as having belonged to her from the beginning.

A year before his death, Rilke wrote to his Polish translator:

> Affirmation of *life-AND-death* turns out to be one in the Elegies. . . . We of the here-and-now are not for a moment satisfied in the world of time, nor are we bound in it; we are continually overflowing toward those who preceded us, toward our origin, and toward those who seemingly come after us. In that vast

"open" world, all beings *are*—one cannot say "contemporaneous," for the very fact that time has ceased determines that they all *are*. Everywhere transience is plunging into the depths of Being. . . . It is our task to imprint this temporary, perishable earth into ourselves so deeply, so painfully and passionately, that its essence can rise again, "invisibly," inside us. We are the bees of the invisible. We wildly collect the honey of the visible, to store it in the great golden hive of the invisible. The Elegies show us at this work, the work of the continual conversion of the beloved visible and tangible world into the invisible vibrations and agitation of our own nature . . . Elegies and Sonnets support each other constantly—, and I consider it an infinite grace that, with the same breath, I was permitted to fill both these sails: the little rust-colored sail of the Sonnets and the Elegies' gigantic white canvas.

(To Witold Hulewicz, November 13, 1925)

The First Elegy (Duino, between January 12 and 16, 1912)

ll. 1 f., *among the angels'/hierarchies:*

"There is really *everything* in the old churches, no shrinking from anything, as there is in the newer ones, where only the 'good' examples appear. Here you see also what is bad and evil and horrible; what is deformed and suffering, what is ugly, what is unjust—and you could say that all this is somehow loved for God's sake. Here is the angel, who doesn't exist, and the devil, who doesn't exist; and the human being, who does exist, stands between them, and (I can't help saying it) their unreality makes him more real to me."

("The Young Workman's Letter," in *Ahead of All Parting*,
Modern Library, 1995, p. 313)

l. 5, *the beginning of terror:*

More and more in my life and in my work I am guided by the effort to correct our old repressions, which have removed and gradually estranged from us the mysteries out of whose abundance our lives might become truly infinite. It is true that these mysteries are dreadful, and people have always drawn away from them. But where can we find anything sweet and glorious that would never wear *this* mask, the mask of the dreadful? Life—and we know nothing else—, isn't life itself dreadful? But as soon as we acknowledge its dreadfulness (not as opponents: what kind of match could we be for it?), but somehow with a confidence that this very dreadfulness may be something completely *ours*, though something that is just now too great, too vast, too incomprehensible for our learning hearts—: as soon as we accept life's most terrifying dreadfulness, at the risk of perishing from it (i.e., from our own Too-much!)—: then an intuition of blessedness will open up for us and, at this cost, will be ours. Whoever does not, sometime or other, give his full consent, his full and *joyous* consent, to the dreadfulness of life, can never take possession of the unutterable abundance and power of our existence; can only walk on its edge, and one day, when the judgment is given, will have been neither alive nor dead. To show the *identity* of dreadfulness and bliss, these two faces on the same divine head, indeed this one *single* face, which just presents itself this way or that, according to our distance from it or the state of mind in which we perceive it—: this is the true significance and purpose of the Elegies and the Sonnets to Orpheus.

(To Countess Margot Sizzo-Noris-Crouy,
April 12, 1923)

l. 13, *our interpreted world:*

> We, *with a word or finger-sign,*
> *gradually make the world our own,*
> *though perhaps its weakest, most precarious part.*
> (Sonnets to Orpheus XVI, First Part)

l. 36, *women in love:*

> Certainly I have no window on human beings. They yield themselves to me only insofar as they take on words within me, and

during these last few years they have been communicating with me almost entirely through two forms, upon which I base my inferences about human beings in general. What speaks to me of humanity—immensely, with a calm authority that fills my hearing with space—is the phenomenon of those who have died young and, even more absolutely, purely, inexhaustibly: *the woman in love*. In these two figures humanity gets mixed into my heart whether I want it to or not. They step forward on my stage with the clarity of the marionette (which is an exterior entrusted with conviction) and, at the same time, as completed types, which nothing can go beyond, so that the definitive natural-history of their souls could now be written.

As for the woman in love (I am not thinking of Saint Theresa or such magnificence of that sort): she yields herself to my observation much more distinctly, purely, i.e., undilutedly and (so to speak) unappliedly in the situation of Gaspara Stampa, Louize Labé, certain Venetian courtesans, and, above all, Marianna Alcoforado, that incomparable creature, in whose eight heavy letters woman's love is for the first time charted from point to point, without display, without exaggeration or mitigation, drawn as if by the hand of a sibyl. And there—my God—there it becomes evident that, as a result of the irresistible logic of woman's heart, this line was finished, perfected, not to be continued any further in the earthly realm, and could be prolonged only toward the divine, into infinity.

(To Annette Kolb, January 23, 1912)

l. 46, *Gaspara Stampa* (1523–1554): An Italian noblewoman who wrote of her unhappy love for Count Collaltino di Collalto in a series of some two hundred sonnets.

l. 63, *those who died young:*

In Padua, where one sees the tombstones of many young men who died there (while they were students at the famous university), in Bologna, in Venice, in Rome, everywhere, I stood as a pupil of death: stood before death's boundless knowledge and let myself be educated. You must also remember how they lie resting in the churches of Genoa and Verona, those youthful forms, not envious of our coming and going, fulfilled within themselves, as if in their death-spasms they had for the first time bitten into the fruit of life, and were now, forever, savoring its unfathomable sweetness.

(To Magda von Hattingberg, February 16, 1914)

l. 67, *Santa Maria Formosa:* A church in Venice, which Rilke had visited in 1911. The reference is to one of the commemorative tablets, inscribed with Latin verses, on the church walls—probably the one that reads (in translation): "I lived for others while life lasted; now, after death, / I have not perished, but in cold marble I live for myself. / I was Willem Hellemans. Flanders mourns me, / Adria sighs for me, poverty calls me. / Died October 16, 1593."

l. 86, *through both realms:*

Death is the *side of life* that is turned away from us and not illuminated. We must try to achieve the greatest possible consciousness of our existence, which is at home in *both these unlimited realms,* and *inexhaustibly nourished by both.* The true form of life extends through *both* regions, the blood of the mightiest circulation pulses through *both:* there *is neither a this-world nor an other-world, but only the great unity,* in which the "angels," those beings who surpass us, are at home.

(To Witold Hulewicz, November 13, 1925)

l. 93, *the lament for Linus:* This ritual lament is mentioned in the *Iliad,* as part of a scene that Hephaestus fashioned on the shield of Achilles:

Girls and young men, with carefree hearts and innocent laughter, were carrying the honey-sweet grapes, piled up in wicker baskets; in their midst, a boy performed the ancient music of yearning, plucking his clear-toned lyre and singing the lament for Linus with his lovely voice, while the others moved to the powerful rhythm, their feet pounding in the dance, leaping and shouting for joy.

(*Iliad* 18, 567 ff.)

According to one myth, Linus was a poet who died young and was mourned by Apollo, his father. Other versions state that he was the greatest poet of all time and was killed by Apollo in a jealous rage; or that he invented music and was the teacher of Orpheus.

The Second Elegy (Duino, late January–early February, 1912)

l. 3, *Tobias:* A young man in the apocryphal Book of Tobit. The story portrays, in passing, the easy, casual contact between a human being and an angel: "And when he went to look for a man to accompany him to Rages, he found Raphael, who was an angel. But Tobias did not know that. . . . And when Tobias had prepared everything necessary for the journey, his father Tobit said, 'Go with this man, and may God prosper your journey, and may the angel of God go with you.' So they both departed, and the young man's dog went along with them."

Tobit 5:4, 16 (in the Codex Vaticanus)

l. 12, *pollen of the flowering godhead:*

> What is shown so beautifully in the world of plants—how they make no secret of their secret, as if they knew that it would always be safe—is exactly what I experienced in front of the sculptures in Egypt and what I have always experienced, ever since, in front of Egyptian Things: this exposure of a secret that is so thoroughly secret, through and through, in every place, that there is no need to hide it. And perhaps everything phallic (as I *fore*-thought in the temple of Karnak, for I couldn't yet think it) is just a setting-forth of the human hidden secret in the sense of the open secret of Nature. I can't remember the smile of the Egyptian gods without thinking of the word "pollen."
>
> (To Lou Andreas-Salomé, February 20, 1914)

ll. 16 f., mirrors: *which scoop up the beauty . . . :*

> The case of the Portuguese nun is so wonderfully pure because she doesn't fling the streams of her emotion on into the imaginary, but rather, with infinite strength, conducts this magnifi-

cent feeling back into herself: enduring *it*, and nothing else. She grows old in the convent, very old; she doesn't become a saint, or even a good nun. It is repugnant to her exquisite tact to apply to God what, from the very beginning, had never been intended for him, and what the Comte de Chamilly could disdain. And yet it was almost impossible to stop the heroic onrush of this love before its final leap: almost impossible, with such a powerful emotion pulsing in her innermost being, not to become a saint. If she—that measurelessly glorious creature— had yielded for even a moment, she would have plunged into God like a stone into the sea. And if it had pleased God to attempt with her what he continually does with the angels, casting all their radiance back into them—: I am certain that, immediately, just as she was, in that sad convent, she would have become an angel, in her deepest self.

(To Annette Kolb, January 23, 1912)

l. 20, *like a perfume:* The reference in the original text is to ambergris or incense burning on a hot coal. (Ernst Zinn, editor's note, SW 1, 792)

ll. 56–59, *you touch so blissfully because . . . / you feel pure duration:* In a letter to Princess Marie about her translation of this Elegy into Italian, Rilke wrote, "I am concerned about this passage, which is so dear to me," and after quoting it, he continued:

This is meant quite literally: that the place where the lover puts his hand is thereby withheld from passing away, from aging, from all the near-disintegration that is always occurring in our integral nature—that simply beneath his hand, this place *lasts, is.* It must be possible, just as literally, to make this clear in Italian; in any paraphrase it is simply lost. Don't you agree? And I think of these lines with a special joy in having been able to write them.

(To Princess Marie von Thurn und Taxis-Hohenlohe, December 16, 1913)

l. 66, *Weren't you astonished:* This is said to the lovers.

ll. 66 f., *the caution of human gestures / on Attic gravestones:*

Once, in Naples I think, in front of some ancient gravestone, it flashed through me that I should never touch people with stronger gestures than the ones depicted there. And I really think that sometimes I get so far as to express the whole impulse of my heart, without loss or destiny, by gently placing my hand on someone's shoulder. Wouldn't that, Lou, wouldn't that be the only progress conceivable within the "restraint" that you ask me to remember?

(To Lou Andreas-Salomé, January 10, 1912)

One of his most definite emotions was to marvel at Greek gravestones of the earliest period: how, upon them, the mutual touching, the resting of hand in hand, the coming of hand to shoulder, was so completely unpossessive. Indeed, it seemed as if in these lingering gestures (which no longer operated in the realm of fate) there was no trace of sadness about a future parting, since the hands were not troubled by any fear of ending or any presentiment of change, since nothing approached them but the long, pure solitude in which they were conscious of themselves as the images of two distant Things that gently come together in the unprovable inner depths of a mirror.

(Notebook entry, early November 1910;
quoted in F.W. Wodtke, *Rilke und Klopstock*,
Kiel diss., 1948, p. 28)

The Third Elegy (The beginning—probably the whole first section—: Duino, January/February 1912; continued and completed in Paris, late autumn 1913)

ll. 26 ff., *Mother, you made him small . . . :*

O night without objects. Dim, outward-facing window; doors that were carefully shut; arrangements from long ago, transmitted, believed in, never quite understood. Silence on the staircase, silence from adjoining rooms, silence high up on the ceiling. O mother: you who are without an equal, who stood before all this silence, long ago in childhood. Who took it upon yourself to say: Don't be afraid; I'm here. Who in the night had the courage to *be* this silence for the child who was frightened, who was dying of fear. You strike a match, and already the noise is you. And you hold the lamp in front of you and say: I'm here; don't be afraid. And you put it down, slowly, and there is no doubt: you are there, you are the light around the familiar, intimate Things, which are there without after-thought, good and simple and sure. And when something moves restlessly in the wall, or creaks on the floor: you just smile, smile transparently against a bright background into the terrified face that looks at you, searching, as if you knew the secret of every half-sound, and everything were agreed and understood between you. Does any power equal your power among the lords of the earth? Look: kings lie and stare, and the teller of tales cannot distract them. Though they lie in the bliss-ful arms of their favorite mistress, horror creeps over them and makes them palsied and impotent. But you come and keep the monstrosity behind you and are entirely in front of it; not like a curtain it can lift up here or there. No: as if you had caught up with it as soon as the child cried out for you. As if you had arrived far ahead of anything that might still happen, and had behind you only your hurrying-in, your eternal path, the flight of your love.

> (*The Notebooks of Malte Laurids Brigge*, New York:
> Random House, 1983, p. 75 f.)


ll. 82, *some confident daily task:*

In the long, complicated solitude in which *Malte* was written, I felt perfectly certain that the strength with which I paid for him originated to a great extent from certain evenings on Capri when nothing happened except that I sat near two elderly women and a girl and watched their needlework, and sometimes at the end was given an apple that one of them had peeled.

> (To Lou Andreas-Salomé, January 10, 1912)

The Fourth Elegy (Munich, November 22–23, 1915)

l. 27, *It at least is full:* This passage was influenced by Heinrich von Kleist's short essay-dialogue "On the Marionette Theater" (1810), which Rilke called "a masterpiece that again and again fills me with astonishment" (To Princess Marie, December 13, 1913). Kleist's character Herr C., in comparing the marionette and the human dancer, says that the marionette has two advantages:

> First of all, a negative one: that it would never behave affectedly. . . . In addition, these puppets have the advantage that they are antigravitational. They know nothing of the inertia of matter, that quality which is most resistant to the dance: because the force that lifts them into the air is greater than the force that binds them to the earth. . . . Puppets need the ground only in order to touch it lightly, like elves, and reanimate the swing of their limbs through this momentary stop. We humans need it to rest on so that we can recover from the exertion of the dance. This moment of rest is clearly no dance in itself; the best we can do with it is to make it as inconspicuous as possible.

l. 35, *the boy with the immovable brown eye:* Rilke's cousin, who died at the age of seven. See note to Sonnets to Orpheus VIII, Second Part, p. 263.

> Beside this lady sat the small son of a female cousin, a boy about as old as I, but smaller and more delicate. His pale, slender neck rose out of a pleated ruff and disappeared beneath a long chin. His lips were thin and closed tightly, his nostrils trembled a bit, and only one of his beautiful dark-brown eyes was movable. It sometimes glanced peacefully and sadly in my direction, while the other eye remained pointed toward the same corner, as if it had been sold and was no longer being taken into account.
>
> (*The Notebooks of Malte Laurids Brigge,* p. 28)

l. 44, *within my deepest hope:*

> As for myself, what has died for me has died, so to speak, into my own heart: when I looked for him, the person who vanished

has collected himself strangely and so surprisingly *in* me, and it was so moving to feel he was now *only* there that my enthusiasm for serving his new existence, for deepening and glorifying it, took the upper hand almost at the very moment when pain would otherwise have invaded and devastated the whole landscape of my spirit. When I remember how I—often with the utmost difficulty in understanding and accepting each other—loved my father! Often, in childhood, my mind became confused and my heart grew numb at the mere thought that someday he might no longer be; my existence seemed to me so wholly conditioned through him (my existence, which from the start was pointed in such a different direction!) that his departure was to my innermost self synonymous with my own destruction . . . , but *so* deeply is death rooted in the essence of love that (if only we are cognizant of death without letting ourselves be misled by the uglinesses and suspicions that have been attached to it) it nowhere contradicts love: *where*, after all, can it drive out someone whom we have carried unsayably in our heart except into this very heart, where would the "idea" of this loved being exist, and his unceasing influence (: for *how* could *that* cease which even while he lived with us was more and more independent of his tangible presence) . . . where would this always secret influence be more secure than *in* us?! Where can we come closer to it, where more purely celebrate it, when obey it better, than when it appears combined with our own voices, as if our heart had learned a new language, a new song, a new strength!

(To Countess Margot Sizzo-Noris-Crouy,
January 6, 1923)

l. 59, *Angel and puppet:* In Kleist's essay the narrator goes on to say that

no matter how cleverly he might present his paradoxes, he would never make me believe that a mechanical marionette could contain more grace than there is in the structure of the human body.

Herr C. replied that, in fact, it is impossible for a human

being to be anywhere near as graceful as a marionette. Only a god can equal inanimate matter in this respect. Here is the point where the two ends of the circular world meet.

I was more and more astonished, and didn't know what I should say to such extraordinary assertions.

It seemed, he said, as he took a pinch of snuff, that I hadn't read the third chapter of the Book of Genesis with sufficient attention; and if a man wasn't familiar with that first period of all human development, one could hardly expect to converse with him about later periods, and certainly not about the final ones.

I told him that I was well aware what disorders consciousness produces in the natural grace of a human being. [Here follow two anecdotes: the first about a young man who by becoming aware of his physical beauty loses it; the second about a pet bear who can easily parry the thrusts of the most accomplished swordsman.]

"Now, my dear fellow," said Herr C., "you are in possession of everything you need in order to understand the point I am making. We see that in the world of Nature, the dimmer and weaker intellect grows, the more radiantly and imperiously grace emerges. But just as a section drawn through two lines, considered from one given point, after passing through infinity, suddenly arrives on the other side of that point; or as the image in a concave mirror, after vanishing into infinity, suddenly reappears right in front of us: so grace too returns when knowledge has, as it were, gone through an infinity. Grace appears most purely in that human form in which consciousness is either nonexistent or infinite, i.e., in the marionette or in the god."

"Does that mean," I said, a bit bewildered, "that we must eat again of the Tree of Knowledge in order to fall back into the state of innocence?"

"Certainly," he answered. "That is the last chapter in the history of the world."

There is a complete translation of the essay in TLS, October 20, 1978.

l. 77, *a pure event*:

> Extensive as the "external" world is, with all its sidereal distances
> it hardly bears comparison with the dimensions, the *depth-
> dimensions*, of our inner being, which does not even need the spa-
> ciousness of the universe to be, in itself, almost unlimited. . . . It
> seems to me more and more as though our ordinary conscious-
> ness inhabited the apex of a pyramid whose base in us (and, as it
> were, beneath us) broadens out to such an extent that the farther
> we are able to let ourselves down into it, the more completely do
> we appear to be included in the realities of earthly and, in the
> widest sense, *worldly*, existence, which are not dependent on
> time and space. From my earliest youth I have felt the intuition
> (and have also, as far as I could, lived by it) that at some deeper
> cross-section of this pyramid of consciousness, mere *being* could
> become an event, the inviolable presence and simultaneity of
> everything that we, on the upper, "normal," apex of self-
> consciousness, are permitted to experience only as entropy.
>
> (To Nora Purtscher-Wydenbruck, August 11, 1924)

The Fifth Elegy (Muzot, February 14, 1922)

This Elegy, the last one to be written, replaced "Antistrophes."

> I had intended to make a copy of the other three Elegies for
> you today, since it is already Sunday again. But now—
> imagine!—in a radiant afterstorm, another Elegy has been
> added, the "Saltimbanques" ["Acrobats"]. It is the most won-
> derful completion; only now does the circle of the Elegies seem
> to me truly closed. It is not added on as the Eleventh, but will
> be inserted (as the Fifth) before the "Hero-Elegy." Besides, the
> piece that previously stood there seemed to me, because of its
> different kind of structure, to be unjustified in that place,
> though beautiful as a poem. The new Elegy will replace it (and
> how!), and the supplanted poem will appear in the section of
> "Fragmentary Pieces" which, as a second part of the book of
> Elegies, will contain everything that is contemporaneous with
> them, all the poems that time, so to speak, destroyed before

they could be born, or cut off in their development to such an extent that the broken edges show.— And so now the "Saltimbanques" too exist, who even from my very first year in Paris affected me so absolutely and have haunted me ever since.

(To Lou Andreas-Salomé, February 19, 1922)

Dedication, *Frau Hertha Koenig:* The owner of Picasso's large ($84'' \times 90\frac{3}{8}''$) 1905 painting *La Famille des Saltimbanques*, which she had bought in December 1914. The painting made such a deep impression on Rilke that he wrote to Frau Koenig asking if he could stay in her Munich home while she was away for the summer of 1915, so that he could live beneath the great work, "which gives me the courage for this request." The request was granted, and Rilke spent four months with the "glorious Picasso."

The other source for the Fifth Elegy is Rilke's experience, over a number of years, with a troupe of Parisian circus people. See "Acrobats," in *Ahead of All Parting*, Modern Library, 1995, p. 288.

l. 14, *the large capital D:* The five standing figures in Picasso's painting seem to be arranged in the shape of a D.

l. 17, *King Augustus the Strong* (1670-1733): King of Poland and elector of Saxony. To entertain his guests at the dinner table, he would, with one hand, crush together a thick pewter plate.

l. 64, *"Subrisio Saltat.":* "Acrobats' Smile." During the printing of the Elegies, Rilke explained this in a note on the proof sheets:

As if it were the label on a druggist's urn; abbreviation of *Subrisio Saltat(orum)*. The labels on these receptacles almost always appear in abbreviated form.

(Ernst Zinn, "Mitteilungen zu R. M. Rilkes Ausgewählten Werken," in *Dichtung und Volkstum* 40, p. 132)

l. 92, *Madame Lamort:* Madame Death.

The Sixth Elegy (Begun at Duino, February/March 1912; lines 1–31: Ronda, January/February 1913; lines 42–44: Paris, late autumn 1913; lines 32–41: Muzot, February 9, 1922)

l. 8, *Like the god stepping into the swan:* Cf. "Leda" (*New Poems*).

l. 20, *Karnak:* Rilke spent two months in Egypt early in 1911 and was deeply moved by

> the incomprehensible temple-world of Karnak, which I saw the very first evening, and again yesterday, under a moon just beginning to wane: saw, saw, saw—my God, you pull yourself together and with all your might you try to believe your two focused eyes—and yet it begins above them, reaches out everywhere above and beyond them (only a god can cultivate such a field of vision) . . .
>
> (To Clara Rilke, January 18, 1911)

In *the team of galloping horses* (1. 19) Rilke is referring to the battle scenes carved on the huge pillars in the Temple of Amun, which depict the pharaoh-generals in their conquering chariots.

l. 31, *Samson:* Judges 13:2, 24; 16:25 ff.

The Seventh Elegy (Muzot, February 7, 1922; lines 87–end: February 26, 1922)

ll. 2 ff., *you would cry out as purely as a bird:*

> The bird is a creature that has a very special feeling of trust in the external world, as if she knew that she is one with its deepest mystery. That is why she sings in it as if she were singing within her own depths; that is why we so easily receive a birdcall into our own depths; we seem to be translating it without residue into our emotion; indeed, it can for a moment turn the whole world into inner space, because we feel that the bird does not distinguish between her heart and the world's.
>
> (To Lou Andreas-Salomé, February 20, 1914)

l. 7, *the silent lover:*

> Learn, inner man, to look on your inner woman,
> the one attained from a thousand
> natures . . .
>
> ("Turning-point," in *Ahead of All Parting*,
> Modern Library, 1995, p. 129)

ll. 34 f., *one earthly Thing / truly experienced:*

These Things, whose essential life you want to express, first ask you, "Are you free? Are you prepared to devote all your love to me, to lie with me as St. Julian the Hospitaller lay beside the leper, giving him the supreme embrace which no simple, fleeting love of one's neighbor could accomplish, because its motive is love, the whole of love, all the love that exists on earth." And if the Thing sees that you are otherwise occupied, with even a particle of your interest, it shuts itself off; it may perhaps give you some slight sign of friendship, a word or a nod, but it will never give you its heart, entrust you with its patient being, its sweet sidereal constancy, which makes it so like the constellations in the sky. In order for a Thing to speak to you, you must regard it for a certain time as *the only one that exists*, as the one and only phenomenon, which through your laborious and exclusive love is now placed at the center of the universe, and which, in that incomparable place, is on that day attended by angels.

(To Baladine Klossowska, December 16, 1920)

l. 36, *Don't think that fate is more than the density of childhood:*

What we call fate does not come to us from outside: it goes forth from within us.

(To Franz Xaver Kappus, August 12, 1904)

l. 37, *how often you outdistanced the man you loved:*

Woman has something of her very own, something suffered, accomplished, perfected. Man, who always had the excuse of being busy with more important matters, and who (let us say it frankly) was not at all adequately prepared for love, has not since antiquity (except for the saints) truly entered into love. The Troubadours knew very well how little they could risk, and Dante, in whom the need became great, only skirted around love with the huge arc of his gigantically evasive poem.

Everything else is, in this sense, derivative and second-rate. . . . You see, after this very salutary interval I am expecting man, the man of the "new heartbeat," who for the time being is getting nowhere, to take upon himself, for the next few thousand years, his own development into the lover—a long, difficult, and, for him, completely new development. As for the woman—withdrawn into the beautiful contour she has made for herself, she will probably find the composure to wait for this slow lover of hers, without getting bored and without too much irony, and, when he arrives, to welcome him.

(To Annette Kolb, January 23, 1912)

l. 71, *in your endless vision:*

For the angel of the Elegies, all the towers and palaces of the past are existent *because* they have long been invisible, and the still-standing towers and bridges of our reality are *already* invisible, although still (for us) physically lasting. . . . All the worlds in the universe are plunging into the invisible as into their next-deeper reality; *a few stars intensify immediately and pass away in the infinite consciousness of the angels—, others are entrusted to beings who slowly and laboriously transform them, in whose terrors and delights they attain their next invisible realization. We,* let it be emphasized once more, *we, in the sense of the Elegies, are these transformers of the earth; our entire existence, the flights and plunges of our love, everything, qualifies us for this task* (beside which there is, essentially, no other).

(To Witold Hulewicz, November 13, 1925)

l. 73, *Pillars:*

. . . a calyx column stands there, alone, a survivor, and you can't encompass it, so far out beyond your life does it reach; only together with the night can you somehow take it in, perceiving it with the stars, as a whole, and then for a second it becomes human—a human experience.

(To Clara Rilke, January 18, 1911)

l. 73, *pylons:* "The monumental gateway to an Egyptian temple, usually formed by two truncated pyramidal towers connected by a lower architectural member containing the gate." (OED)

l. 73, *the Sphinx:* See note to the Tenth Elegy, ll. 73 ff., pp. 246 ff.

l. 84, *a woman in love—, oh alone at night by her window:* Cf. "Woman in Love" (*New Poems*).

l. 87, *filled with departure:*

> I sometimes wonder whether longing can't radiate out from someone so powerfully, like a storm, that nothing can come to him from the opposite direction. Perhaps William Blake has somewhere drawn that—?
>
> (To Princess Marie von Thurn und Taxis-Hohenlohe,
> May 14, 1912)

The Eighth Elegy (Muzot, February 7/8, 1922)

Dedication, *Rudolf Kassner:* Austrian writer (1873–1959).

l. 2, *into the Open:*

> You must understand the concept of the "Open," which I have tried to propose in this Elegy, as follows: The animal's degree of consciousness is such that it comes into the world without at every moment setting the world over against itself (as we do). The animal is *in* the world; we stand *in front of* the world because of the peculiar turn and heightening which our consciousness has taken. So by the "Open" it is not sky or air or space that is meant; they, too, for the human being who observes and judges, are "objects" and thus "opaque" and closed. The animal or the flower presumably *is* all that, without accounting for itself, and therefore has before itself and above itself that indescribably open freedom which has its

(extremely fleeting) equivalents for us perhaps only in the first moments of love, when we see our own vastness in the person we love, and in the ecstatic surrender to God.

> (To Lev P. Struve, February 25, 1926, in Maurice Betz,
> *Rilke in Frankreich: Erinnerungen—Briefe—Dokumente*,
> Wien / Leipzig / Zürich:
> Herbert Reichner Verlag, 1937)

ll. 2 f., *Only our eyes are turned / backward:* In describing his experience of "reaching the other side of Nature," Rilke uses the mirror image of this metaphor:

> Altogether, he was able to observe how all objects yielded themselves to him more distantly and, at the same time, somehow more truly; this might have been due to his own vision, which was no longer directed forward and diluted in empty space; he was looking, as if over his shoulder, *backward* at Things, and their now completed existence took on a bold, sweet aftertaste, as though everything had been spiced with a trace of the blossom of parting.
>
> ("An Experience," in *Ahead of All Parting*,
> Modern Library, 1995, p. 291)

l. 9, *Free from death:*

> Nearby there was one of the darker birdcalls, a more mature one, already sung inwardly, which was to the others as a poem is to a few words—how it shone toward God, already, already, how devout it was, how filled with itself, a song-bud still in the calyx of its sound, but already aware of its own irrepressible fullness, pre-blissful and pre-afraid. Or rather, the fear was entirely there, the indivisible pain common to all creatures, which is as simple as the blissfulness over there, on the other side, where all has been surmounted.
>
> (To Nanny Wunderly-Volkart,
> February 24, 1920)

l. 13, *fountain:* Here, as well as in the Ninth Elegy, l. 33, and Sonnets to Orpheus VIII, First Part, this is meant in its older sense of "a spring or source of water issuing from the earth and collecting in a basin, natural or artificial; also, the head-spring or source of a stream or river." (OED)

l. 53 ff., *Oh bliss of the* tiny *creature . . . :*

> That a multitude of creatures which come from externally exposed seeds have *that* as their maternal body, that vast sensitive freedom—how much at home they must feel in it all their lives; in fact they do nothing but leap for joy in their mother's womb, like little John the Baptist; for this same space has both conceived them and brought them forth, and they never leave its security.
>
> Until in the bird everything becomes a little more uneasy and cautious. The nest that Nature has given him is already a small maternal womb, which he only covers instead of wholly containing it. And suddenly, as if it were no longer safe enough outside, the wonderful maturing flees wholly into the darkness of the creature and emerges into the world only at a later turning-point, experiencing it as a second world and never entirely weaned from the conditions of the earlier, more intimate one.
>
> (Rivalry between mother and world—)
>
> (Notebook entry, February 20, 1914;
>
> SW 6, 1074 f.)

The Ninth Elegy (Lines 1–6a and 77–79: Duino, March 1912; the rest: Muzot, February 9, 1922)

l. 7, *happiness:*

> The reality of any joy in the world is indescribable; only in joy does creation take place (happiness, on the contrary, is only a promising, intelligible constellation of things already there); joy is a marvelous increasing of what exists, a pure addition

out of nothingness. How superficially must happiness engage us, after all, if it can leave us time to think and worry about how long it will last. Joy is a moment, unobligated, timeless from the beginning, not to be held but also not to be truly lost again, since under its impact our being is changed chemically, so to speak, and does not only, as may be the case with happiness, savor and enjoy itself in a new mixture.

(To Ilse Erdmann, January 31, 1914)

ll. 9 f., *the heart, which / would exist in the laurel too:*

Hardly had she cried her breathless prayer
when a numbness seized her body; her soft breasts
were sealed in bark, her hair turned into leaves,
her arms into branches; her feet, which had been so quick,
plunged into earth and rooted her to the spot.
Only her shining grace was left. Apollo
still loved her; he reached out his hand to touch
the laurel trunk, and under the rough bark
could feel her heart still throbbing . . .

(Ovid, Metamorphoses I, 548 ff.)

ll. 32 ff., *house, / bridge . . . :*

Even for our grandparents a "house," a "well," a familiar tower, their very clothes, their coat, was infinitely more, infinitely more intimate; almost everything was a vessel in which they found what is human and added to the supply of what is human.

(To Witold Hulewicz, November 13, 1925)

l. 59, *the rope-maker in Rome or the potter along the Nile:*

I often wonder whether things unemphasized in themselves haven't exerted the most profound influence on my development and my work: the encounter with a dog; the hours I spent in Rome watching a rope-maker, who in his craft repeated one of the oldest gestures in the world—as did the potter in a little village on the Nile; standing beside his wheel was indescribably and in a most mysterious sense fruitful for me. . . .

(To Alfred Schaer, February 26, 1924)

ll. 68 f., *to arise within us,* / invisible:

The Spanish landscape (the last one that I experienced absolutely), Toledo, pushed this attitude of mine to its extreme limit: because there the external Thing itself—tower, mountain, bridge—already possessed the extraordinary, unsurpassable intensity of those inner equivalents through which one might have wished to represent it. Everywhere appearance and vision merged, as it were, in the object; in each one of them a whole inner world was revealed, as though an angel who encompassed all space were blind and gazing into himself. This, a world seen no longer from the human point of view, but inside the angel, is perhaps my real task—one, at any rate, in which all my previous attempts would converge.

(To Ellen Delp, October 27, 1915)

l. 77, *our intimate companion, Death:*

We should not be afraid that our strength is insufficient to endure any experience of death, even the closest and most ter-rifying. Death is not *beyond* our strength; it is the measuring-line at the vessel's brim: we are *full* whenever we reach it—and being full means (for us) being heavy.—I am not saying that we should *love* death; but we should love life so generously, so without calculation and selection, that we involuntarily come to include, and to love, death too (life's averted half); this is in fact what always happens in the great turmoils of love, which cannot be held back or defined. Only because we exclude death, when it suddenly enters our thoughts, has it become more and more of a stranger to us; and because we have kept it a stranger, it has become our enemy. It is conceivable that it is infinitely closer to us than life itself—. What do we know of it?!

Prejudiced as we are against death, we do not manage to release it from all its distorted images. It is a *friend,* our deepest friend, perhaps the only one who can never be misled by our attitudes and vacillations—and this, you must understand, *not* in the sentimental-romantic sense of life's opposite, a denial of life: but our friend precisely when we most passionately, most vehemently, assent to being here, to living and working on earth, to Nature, to love. Life simultaneously says Yes and No. Death (I implore you to believe this!) is the true Yes-sayer. It says *only* Yes. In the presence of eternity.

(To Countess Margot Sizzo-Noris-Crouy,
January 6, 1923)

The Tenth Elegy (Lines 1–12: Duino, January/February 1912; continued in Paris, late autumn 1913; new conclusion, lines 13–end: Muzot, February 11, 1922)

Lou, dear Lou, finally:
At this moment, Saturday, the eleventh of February, at 6 o'clock, I am putting down my pen after completing the last Elegy, the Tenth. The one (even then it was intended as the last one) whose first lines were already written in Duino: "Someday, emerging at last from the violent insight, / let me sing out jubilation and praise to assenting angels. . . . " What there was of it I once read to you; but only the first twelve lines have remained, all the rest is new and: yes, very, very glorious!—Imagine! I have been allowed to survive until this. Through everything. Miracle. Grace.

(To Lou Andreas-Salomé, February 11, 1922)

l. 20, *market of solace:*

Consolation is one of the many diversions we are subject to, a distraction, hence something essentially frivolous and unfruitful.—Even time doesn't "console," as people superficially say, at most it arranges, it sets in order—, and only because we later pay so little attention to the order toward which it so quietly collaborates that instead of marveling at what is now established and assuaged, reconciled in the great whole, we think it is some forgetfulness of our own, some weakness of heart, just because it no longer hurts us so much. Ah, how little the heart really forgets it,—and how strong it would be if we didn't withdraw its tasks from it before they are fully and truly accomplished!—Our instinct shouldn't be to want to console ourselves for such a loss, rather it should become our deep and painful curiosity to wholly explore it, the particularity, the uniqueness of precisely *this* loss, to discover its effect within our life, indeed we should summon up the noble avarice of enriching our inner world by precisely *it*, by its meaning and heaviness ... The more deeply such a loss touches us and the more intensely it affects us, the more it becomes a *task*, of newly, differently, and finally taking into our possession what now, in its being lost, is accented with hopelessness: *this* then is unending accomplishment which immediately overcomes all negative qualities that cling to pain, all laziness and indulgence that always constitute a part of pain, this is active, inward-working pain, the only kind that makes sense and is worthy of us. I don't like the Christian ideas of a Beyond, I am getting farther and farther away from them, naturally without any thought of attacking them—; they may have a right to their existence beside so many other hypotheses about the divine periphery,—but for me they contain above all the danger not only of making those who have vanished more indistinct to us and above all more inaccessible—; but also we ourselves, because we allow our longing to pull us *away* from here, thereby become less definite, less earthly: which nevertheless, for the present, as long as we are *here* and related to tree, flower, and soil, we in a purest sense have to remain, even still have to become! ... I reproach all modern religions for having provided their believers with consolations and glossings-over of death, instead of giving them the means of coming to an understanding with it. With it and with its full, unmasked cruelty: this cruelty is so immense that it is precisely with *it* that the circle closes: it leads back into a mildness which is greater, purer, and more perfectly clear (all consolation is muddy!) than we have ever, even on the sweetest spring day, imagined mildness to be. But toward the experiencing of this deepest mildness, which, if even a few of us were to feel it with conviction, could perhaps little by little penetrate and make transparent all the relations of life: toward the experiencing of *this* most rich and complete mildness mankind has never taken even the first steps,—unless in its most ancient, most innocent ages, whose secret is all but lost to us. The content of the "initiations" was, I am sure, nothing but the communicating of a "key" that allowed people to read the word "death" *without* negation; like the moon, surely life has a side permanently turned away from us which is *not* its opposite but its counterpart toward completion, toward wholeness, toward the actual perfect and full sphere and globe of *being*.

(To Countess Margot Sizzo-Noris-Crouy,
January 6, 1923)

l. 21, *the church:*

The Christian experience enters less and less into consideration; the primordial God outweighs it infinitely. The idea that we are sinful and need to be redeemed as a prerequisite for God is more and more repugnant to a heart that has comprehended the earth. Sin is the most wonderfully roundabout path to God—but why should *they* go wandering who have never left him? The strong, inwardly quivering bridge of the Mediator has meaning only where the abyss between God and us is admitted—; but this very abyss is full of the darkness of God; and where someone experiences it, let him climb down and howl away inside it (that is more necessary than crossing it). Not until we can make even the abyss our dwelling-place will the paradise that we have sent on ahead of us turn around and will everything deeply and fervently of the here-and-now, which the Church embezzled for the Beyond, come back to us; then all the angels will decide, singing praises, in favor of the earth!

(To Ilse Jahr, February 22, 1923)

l. 62, *the vast landscape of Lament:*

The land of Lament, through which the elder Lament guides
the dead youth, is *not* to be *identified* with Egypt, but is only, as
it were, a reflection of the Nile-land in the desert clarity of the
consciousness of the dead.

(To Witold Hulewicz, November 13, 1925)

ll. 73–88, *But as night approaches . . . / . . . the indescribable outline:*

Go look at the Head of Amenophis the Fourth in the Egyptian
Museum in Berlin; feel, in this face, what it means to be oppo-
site the infinite world and, within such a limited surface,
through the intensified arrangement of a few features, to form
a weight that can balance the whole universe. Couldn't one
turn away from a starry night to find the same law blossoming
in this face, the same grandeur, depth, inconceivableness? By
looking at such Things I learned to see; and when, later, in
Egypt, many of them stood before me, in their extreme indi-
viduality, insight into them poured over me in such waves that
I lay for almost a whole night beneath the great Sphinx, as
though I had been vomited out in front of it by my whole life.

You must realize that it is difficult to be alone there; it has
become a public square; the most irrelevant foreigners are
dragged in *en masse.* But I had skipped dinner; even the Arabs
were sitting at a distance, around their fire; one of them noticed
me, but I got away by buying two oranges from him; and then
the darkness hid me. I had waited for nightfall out in the desert,
then I came in slowly, the Sphinx at my back, figuring that the
moon must already be rising (for there was a full moon) behind
the nearest pyramid, which was glowing intensely in the sunset.
And when at last I had come around it, not only was the moon
already far up in the sky, but it was pouring out such a stream of
brightness over the endless landscape that I had to dim its light
with my hand, in order to find my way among the heaps of rub-
ble and the excavations. I found a place to sit down on a slope
near the Sphinx, opposite that gigantic form, and I lay there,
wrapped in my coat, frightened, unspeakably taking part. I don't
know whether my existence ever emerged so completely into

consciousness as during those night hours when it lost all value: for what was it in comparison with all that? The dimension in which it moved had passed into darkness; everything that is world and existence was happening on a higher plane, where a star and a god lingered in silent confrontation. You too can undoubtedly remember experiencing how the view of a landscape, of the sea, of the great star-flooded night inspires us with the sense of connections and agreements beyond our understanding. It was precisely this that I experienced, to the highest degree; here there arose an image built on the pattern of the heavens; upon which thousands of years had had no effect aside from a little contemptible decay; and most incredible of all was that this Thing had human features (the fervently recognizable features of a human face) and that, in such an exalted position, these features were enough. Ah, my dear—I said to myself, "This, this, which we alternately thrust into fate and hold in our own hands: it must be capable of some great significance if even in such surroundings its form can persist." This face had taken on the customs of the universe; single parts of its gaze and smile were damaged, but the rising and setting of the heavens had mirrored into it emotions that had endured. From time to time I closed my eyes and, though my heart was pounding, I reproached myself for not experiencing this deeply enough; wasn't it necessary to reach places in my astonishment where I had never been before? I said to myself, "Imagine, you could have been carried here blindfolded and been set down on a slope in the deep, barely-stirring coolness—you wouldn't have known where you were and you would have opened your eyes—" And when I really did open them, dear God: it took quite a long time for them to endure it, to take in this immense being, to achieve the mouth, the cheek, the forehead, upon which moonlight and moonshadows passed from expression to expression. How many times already had my eyes attempted this full cheek; it rounded itself out so slowly that there seemed to be room up there for *more* places than in our world. And then, as I gazed at it, I was suddenly, unexpectedly, taken into its confidence, I received a knowledge of that cheek, experienced it in the perfect emotion of its curve. For a few moments I didn't grasp what had happened. Imagine: this: Behind the great projecting crown on the Sphinx's head, an owl had flown up and had slowly, indescribably *audibly* in the pure depths of the night, brushed the face with her faint flight: and now, upon my hearing, which had grown very acute in the hours-long nocturnal silence, the outline of that cheek was (as though by a miracle) inscribed.

(To Magda von Hattingberg, February 1, 1914)

l. 108, *hazel-trees:* Rilke had originally written "willows"; this was corrected on the advice of a friend, who sent him a small handbook of trees and shrubs.

What a kind thought it was of yours to introduce me so clearly and thoroughly to the elements of "catkinology" with your book and the explanatory letter; after this there is no need for further or more exact information: I am convinced! So (remarkably enough) there are no "hanging" willow catkins; and even if there were some rare, tropical exception, I still would not be able to use it. The place in the poem that I wanted to check for factual accuracy stands or falls according to whether the reader can understand, with his *first* intuition, precisely this *falling* of the catkins; otherwise, the image loses all meaning. So the absolutely *typical* appearance of this inflorescence must be evoked—and I immediately realized from the very instructive illustrations in your little book that the shrub which, years ago, supplied me with the impression I have now used in my work must have been a hazelnut tree; whose branches are furnished most densely, *before* the leaves come out, with long, perpendicularly hanging catkins. So I know what I needed to know and have changed the text from "willow" to "hazel."

(To Elisabeth Aman-Volkart, June 1922)

## APPENDIX TO DUINO ELEGIES

[Fragment of an Elegy] (Duino, late January 1912)

Written between the First and Second Elegies.

[Original Version of the Tenth Elegy] (Lines 1–15: Duino, January / February 1912; continued in Paris, late in 1913)

Antistrophes (Lines 1–4: Venice, summer 1912; the rest: Muzot, February 9, 1922)

See note to the Fifth Elegy, p. 233.

*Antistrophe:* "The returning movement, from left to right, in Greek choruses and dances, answering to the previous movement of the strophe from right to left; hence, the lines of choral song recited during this movement." (OED)

## THE SONNETS TO ORPHEUS (1923)

These strange Sonnets were no intended or expected work; they appeared, often *many* in one day (the first part of the book was written in about three days), completely unexpectedly, in February of last year, when I was, moreover, about to gather myself for the continuation of those other poems—the great Duino Elegies. I could do nothing but submit, purely and obediently, to the dictation of this inner impulse; and I understood only little by little the relation of these verses to the figure of Vera Knoop, who died at the age of eighteen or nineteen, whom I hardly knew and saw only a few times in her life, when she was still a child, though with extraordinary attention and emotion. Without my arranging it this way (except for a few poems at the beginning of the second part, all the Sonnets kept the chronological order of their appearance), it happened that only the next-to-last poems of both parts explicitly refer to Vera, address her, or evoke her figure.

This beautiful child, who had just begun to dance and attracted the attention of everyone who saw her, by the art of movement and transformation which was innate in her body and spirit—unexpectedly declared to her mother that she no longer could or would dance (this happened just at the end of childhood). Her body changed, grew strangely heavy and massive, without losing its beautiful Slavic features; this was already the beginning of the mysterious glandular disease that later was to bring death so quickly. During the time that remained to her, Vera devoted herself to music; finally she only drew—as if the denied dance came forth from her ever more quietly, ever more discreetly.

(To Countess Margot Sizzo-Noris-Crouy, April 12, 1923)

I myself have only now, little by little, comprehended them and found a way to pass them on;—with brief comments that I insert when I read them aloud, I am able to make the whole more intelligible; interconnections are established everywhere, and where a darkness remains, it is the kind of darkness that requires not clarification but surrender.

(To Clara Rilke, April 23, 1923)

. . . *we, in the sense of the Elegies, are these transformers of the earth; our entire existence, the flights and plunges of our love, everything, qualifies us for this task* (beside which there is, essentially, no other). (The Sonnets show particular examples of this activity, which appears in them, placed under the name and protection of a dead girl, whose incompletion and innocence holds open the grave-door so that, having passed on, she belongs to those powers which keep the one half of life fresh, and open toward the other, wound-open half.)

(To Witold Hulewicz, November 13, 1925)

I say "sonnets." Though they are the freest, most (as it were) conjugated poems that have ever been included under this usually so motionless and stable form. But precisely this—to conjugate the sonnet, to intensify it, to give it the greatest possible scope without destroying it—was for me a strange experiment: which, in any case, I made no conscious decision to undertake. So strongly was it imposed, so fully did it contain its solution in itself.

(To Katharina Kippenberg, February 23, 1922)

Today just one favor more, which I have been wanting to ask of you for a long time: could you eventually have printed for me one copy of the "Sonnets to Orpheus," and perhaps also one copy of the "Elegies," interleaved with blank pages, using paper that can absorb good ink without making it "bleed"? I would like to append brief commentaries here and there to the more difficult poems, for my own use and for the benefit of a few friends; it would be a curious work, in which I would strangely have to account for the place of this verse within my own inner proportions. Whether or not that happens, I would in any case be glad to have both books, especially the "Sonnets," prepared in this way, so that I can make notes in it whenever I feel the inclination. (There is no hurry, of course!)

(To Anton Kippenberg, March 11, 1926)

FIRST PART

I (Muzot, February 2/5, 1922)

II (Muzot, February 2/5, 1922)

l. 1, *almost a girl:*

Siehe, innerer Mann, dein inneres Mädchen

*Look, inner man, at your inner girl*

("Turning-point,"in *Ahead of All Parting,*
Modern Library, 1995, p. 129)

The deepest experience of the creative artist is feminine, for it is an experience of conceiving and giving birth. The poet Obstfelder once wrote, speaking of the face of a stranger: "When he began to speak, it was as though a *woman* had taken a seat within him." It seems to me that every poet has had that experience in beginning to speak.

(To a young woman, November 20, 1904)

III (Muzot, February 2/5, 1922)

ll. 3f., *crossing / of heart-roads:* "The sanctuaries that stood at crossroads in classical antiquity were dedicated to sinister deities like Hecate, not to Apollo, the bright god of song." (Hermann Mörchen, *Rilkes Sonette an Orpheus*, Stuttgart: W. Kohlhammer Verlag, 1958, p. 66)

l. 13, *True singing:*

> It is not only the *hearable* in music that is important (something can be pleasant to hear without being *true*). What is decisive for me, in all the arts, is not their outward appearance, not what is called the "beautiful"; but rather their deepest, most inner origin, the buried reality that calls forth their appearance.
>
> (To Princess Marie von Thurn und Taxis-Hohenlohe, November 17, 1912)

l. 14, *A gust inside the god. A wind.:*

> All in a few days, it was a nameless storm, a hurricane in the spirit (like that time at Duino), everything that was fiber and fabric in me cracked.
>
> (Ibid., February 11, 1922, just after the completion of the Elegies)

> Never have I gone through such tremendous gales of being-taken-hold-of: I was an element, Liliane, and could do everything elements can do.
>
> (To Claire Studer-Goll, April 11, 1923)

IV (Muzot, February 2/5, 1922)

V (Muzot, February 2/5, 1922)

l. 5, *It is Orpheus once for all:*

> Ultimately there is only *one* poet, that infinite one who makes himself felt, here and there through the ages, in a mind that can surrender to him.
>
> (To Nanny Wunderly-Volkart, July 29, 1920)

True art can issue only from a purely anonymous center.
(To R. S., November 22, 1920)

VI (Muzot, February 2/5, 1922)

l. 2, *both realms:*

Angels (they say) don't know whether it is the living
they are moving among, or the dead. The eternal torrent
whirls all ages along in it, through both realms
forever, and their voices are drowned out in its thunderous roar.
(The First Elegy, ll. 92 ff.)

l. 4, *willow-branch:* From Psalm 137, to Desdemona's song, to modern
poetry, the willow has been a symbol of grief. Its association with the dead
goes back at least as far as Homer:

But when the North Wind has breathed you across the River
of Ocean,
you will come to a wooded coast and the Grove of Persephone,
dense with shadowy poplars and willows that shed their seeds.
Beach your boat on that shore as the ocean-tide foams behind
you;
then walk ahead by yourself, into the Land of Decay.
(Odyssey X, 508 ff.)

l. 10, *earthsmoke and rue:* Herbs used in summoning the dead.

But slowly growing beside it is patience, that delicate "earth-
smoke."
(To Gudi Nölke, October 5, 1919)

l. 11, *connection:*

The comprehensible slips away, is transformed; instead of
possession one learns connection.
(To Ilse Jahr, February 22, 1923)

VII (Muzot, February 2/5, 1922)

l. 9, *decay in the sepulcher of kings:*

> It is true, the gods have neglected no opportunity of exposing us: they let us uncover the great kings of Egypt in their tombs, and we were able to see them in their natural decay, how they were spared no indignity.
>
> ("On the Young Poet," in *Ahead of All Parting*,
> Modern Library, 1995, p. 293 f.)

VIII (Muzot, February 2/5, 1922)

IX (Muzot, February 2/5, 1922)

X (Muzot, February 2/5, 1922)

l. 2, *coffins of stone:* Used as troughs or basins in the fountains of Italian towns.

> Da wurde von den alten Aquädukten
> ewiges Wasser in sie eingelenkt . . .
>
> *Then, eternal water from the ancient*
> *aqueducts was channeled into them . . .*
> ("Roman Sarcophagi," *New Poems*)

l. 5, *those other ones:*

> (what is being referred to, after the Roman ones, are those other, uncovered sarcophagi in the famous cemetery of Aliscamps, out of which flowers bloom)
>
> —Rilke's note

l. 6, *shepherd:* See "The Spanish Trilogy," in *Ahead of All Parting*, Modern Library, 1995, pp. 103 f.

l. 7, *bee-suck nettle: Lamium album,* white dead-nettle.

XI (Muzot, February 2/5, 1922)

l. 1, "*Rider*":

> —Look, there:
> the *Rider*, the *Staff*, and the larger constellation called *Garland*
> *of Fruit*.
>
> (The Tenth Elegy, p. 67.)

XII (Muzot, February 2/5, 1922)

l. 7, *antennas:*

> Oh how she [Vera] loved, how she reached out with the anten-
> nas of her heart beyond everything that is comprehensible and
> embraceable here— . . .
>
> (To Gertrud Ouckama Knoop, January 1922)

XIII (Muzot, February 2/5, 1922)

> Comme le fruit se fond en jouissance,
> Comme en délice il change son absence
> Dans une bouche où sa forme se meurt, . . .
>
> (Valéry, "Le Cimetière Marin")

> *So wie die Frucht sich auflöst im Genusse,*
> *Abwesenheit Entzücken wird zum Schlusse*
> *in einem Mund, drin ihre Form verschwand, . . .*
>
> (Rilke's translation,
> March 14 and 16, 1921)

l. 9, "*apple*":

> At various times I have had the experience of feeling apples,
> more than anything else—barely consumed, and often while I

was still eating them—being transposed into spirit. Thus perhaps the Fall. (If there *was* one.)

(To Princess Marie von Thurn und Taxis-Hohenlohe,
January 16, 1912)

XIV (Muzot, February 2/5, 1922)

XV (Muzot, February 2/5, 1922)

XVI (Muzot, February 2/5, 1922)

One has to know—or guess—that Sonnet XVI is addressed to a dog; I didn't want to add a note to this effect, precisely -because I wanted to take him completely into the whole. Any hint would just have isolated him again, singled him out. (This way he takes part down below, belonging and warned, like the dog and the child in Rembrandt's Night Watch.)

(To Clara Rilke, April 23, 1923)

Now it is my turn to thank you, not for Pierrot, for God's sake *no:* it would be his ruin, Pierrot's ruin, the saddest story in the world. How could you even think I might adopt him, what kind of match could I be for his boundless homesickness? Furthermore, apart from the torment of helplessly looking on, I would have the additional torment of sacrificing myself for his sake, which I find especially painful where dogs are involved: they touch me so deeply, these beings who are entirely dependent on us, whom we have helped up to a soul for which there is no heaven. Even though I need all of my heart, it is probable that this would end, end tragically, by my breaking off little pieces from the edge of it at first, then bigger and bigger pieces toward the middle (like dog biscuits) for this Pierrot as he cried for you and no longer understood life; I would, after hesitating for a little while, give up my writing and live entirely for his consolation.

(To N. N., February 8, 1912)

l. 7, *You know the dead:*

"And I was about to (I feel quite cold, Malte, when I think of it), but, God help me, I was just about to say, 'Where is . . .'— when Cavalier shot out from under the table, as he always did, and ran to meet her. I saw it, Malte; I saw it. He ran toward her, although she wasn't coming; for him she *was* coming." ·

(*The Notebooks of Malte Laurids Brigge*, p. 89)

ll. 11f., *don't plant / me inside your heart:*

"In the end a responsibility would arise, which I can't accept. You wouldn't notice how completely you had come to trust me; you would overvalue me and expect from me what I can't perform. You would watch me and approve of everything, even of what is unworthy. If I want to give you a joy: will I find one? And if one day you are sad and complain to me—will I be able to help you?—And you shouldn't think that *I* am the one who lets you die. Go away, I beg of you: go away."

("A Meeting," in *Ahead of All Parting*,
Modern Library, 1995, p. 285)

l. 13, my *master's hand:*

In the poem *to the dog*, by "my master's hand" the hand of the god is meant; here, of "Orpheus." The poet wants to guide this hand so that it too may, for the sake of his [the dog's] infinite sympathy and devotion, bless the dog, who, almost like Esau, has put on his pelt only so that he could share, in his heart, an inheritance that would never come to him: could participate, with sorrow and joy, in all of human existence.

(To Countess Margot Sizzo-Noris-Crouy,
June 1, 1923)

XVII (Muzot, February 2/5, 1922)

XVIII (Muzot, February 2/5, 1922)

XIX (Muzot, February 2/5, 1922)

XX (Muzot, February 2/5, 1922)

> And imagine, one thing *more*, in another connection (in the "Sonnets to Orpheus," twenty-five sonnets, written, suddenly, in the prestorm, as a monument for Vera Knoop), I wrote, *made*, the *horse*, you know, the free happy white horse with the hobble on his foot, who once, as evening fell, on a Volga meadow, came bounding toward us at a gallop—:
>
> how
>
> I made him, as an "ex-voto" for Orpheus!—What is time?—*When* is Now? Across so many years he bounded, with his absolute happiness, into my wide-open feeling.
>
> (To Lou Andreas-Salomé, February 11, 1922)

There is also an account of the incident in Lou Andreas-Salomé's travel diary:

> As we were standing by the Volga, a neigh resounded through the silent evening, and a frisky little horse, having finished its day of work, came quickly trotting toward the herd, which was spending the night somewhere, far away, in the meadow-steppes. In the distance one could now and then see the shepherds' fire blazing in the clear night. After a while a second little horse, from somewhere else, followed, more laboriously: they had tied a wooden hobble to one of his legs, in order to stop him from wildly leaping into the wheatfield.
>
> (*Briefwechsel*, p. 611)

l. 13, *cycle of myths:*

> It is done, *done!* / The blood- and myth-cycle of ten (ten!) strange years has been completed.—It was (now for the first time I feel it entirely) like a mutilation of my heart, that this did not exist. And now it is here.
>
> (To Nanny Wunderly-Volkart, February 10, 1922)

XXI (Muzot, February 9, 1922; inserted here as a replacement for the original sonnet; see p. 197)

> The little spring-song seems to me, as it were, an "interpretation" of a remarkable, dancing music that I once heard sung by the convent children at a morning Mass in the little church at Ronda (in southern Spain). The children, who kept leaping to a dance rhythm, sang a text I didn't know, to the accompaniment of triangle and tambourine.
>
> —Rilke's note*

If the Sonnets to Orpheus were allowed to reach publication, probably two or three of them, which, I now see, just served as conduits for the stream (e.g., the XXIst) and after its passage-through remained empty, would have to be replaced by others.
(To Gertrud Ouckama Knoop, February 7, 1922)

It makes me uncomfortable to think of that XXIst poem, the "empty" one in which the "transmissions" appear ("The New, my friends, is not a matter of") . . . , please paste it over, right now, with this child's-spring-song, written today, which, I think, enriches the sound of the whole cycle and stands fairly well, as a pendant, opposite the white horse.

This little song, which had risen into my consciousness when I woke up this morning, fully formed up to the eighth line, and the rest of it immediately afterward, appears to me like an interpretation of a "Mass"—a real *Mass*, gaily accompanied as if with hanging garlands of sound: the convent children sang it to I don't know what text, but in this dance-step, in the little nuns'-church at Ronda (in southern Spain—); sang it, one can hear, to tambourine and triangle!—It fits, doesn't it, into these interrelationships of the Sonnets to Orpheus: as the brightest spring-tone in them? (I think it does.)

---

* This and the note to Sonnet XI, Second Part are the only two notes Rilke himself ever published. The others marked "Rilke's note" were handwritten in a copy of the Sonnets which he sent to Herr and Frau Leopold von Schlözer on May 30, 1923.

(Does the paper more-or-less match? I hope it is the same.)
Only this—and only because that XXIst is like a blot on my conscience.

(To Gertrud Ouckama Knoop, February 9, 1922)

XXII (Muzot, February 2/5, 1922)

XXIII (Muzot, February 13, 1922)

This Sonnet I have—at least temporarily—inserted as the XXIII, so that what has become the *first* part of the Sonnets now contains twenty-six poems.

(To Gertrud Ouckama Knoop, March 18, 1922)

XXIV (Muzot, February 2/5, 1922)

XXV (Muzot, February 2/5, 1922)

(to Vera)

—Rilke's note

XXVI (Muzot, February 2/5, 1922)

l. 2, *rejected:*

> Three years went by, but Orpheus still refused
> to love another woman: so intense
> his grief was, for his lost Eurydice;
> or else because he had vowed to stay alone.
> But many women desired him, and raged
> at his abrupt rejection.
>
> (Ovid, Metamorphoses X, 78 ff.)

l. 2, *attacked:*

> From a nearby hill the frenzied women, bristling
> in skins of savage beasts, at last caught sight
> of Orpheus, as he sat absorbed in music,
> accompanied by the sweet lyre. One of them,

her long hair streaming in the wind, cried out:
"Look! there he is, that man who shows us such
contempt." And, with a yell, she hurled her spear
straight at the singing mouth . . .

(Ibid. XI, 3 ff.)

l. 5, *could not destroy your head or your lyre:*

His limbs lay scattered; but the river Hebrus
took the head and lyre, and as they floated
down its stream, the lyre began to play
a mournful tune, and the lifeless tongue sang out
mournfully, and both the river-banks
answered, with their own, faint, mournful echo.

(Ibid. XI, 50 ff.)

l. 7, *stones:*

Another threw a stone; but in mid-flight,
overwhelmed by the beauty of the song,
it fell at his feet, as though to beg forgiveness
for its violent intention.

(Ibid. XI, 10 ff.)

l. 9, *At last they killed you:*

Such music would have moved to softness all
these stones and spears; except that the wild shrieking,
shrill flutes, the blare of trumpets, drumbeats, howls
of the enraged bacchantes had completely
drowned out the lyre's voice. Until at last
the unhearing stones reddened with poet's blood.

(Ibid. XI, 15 ff.)

SECOND PART

I (Muzot, approximately February 23, 1922; the last of the Sonnets to
be written)

II (Muzot, February 15/17, 1922)

III (Muzot, February 15/17, 1922)

l. 7, *sixteen-pointer:* A large stag, with sixteen points or branches to its antlers.

IV (Muzot, February 15/17, 1922)

> Any "allusion," I am convinced, would contradict the inde-
> scribable *presence* of the poem. So in the unicorn no parallel
> with Christ is intended; rather, all love of the non-proven, the
> non-graspable, all belief in the value and reality of whatever
> our heart has through the centuries created and lifted up out
> of itself: that is what is praised in this creature. . . . The uni-
> corn has ancient associations with virginity, which were con-
> tinually honored during the Middle Ages. Therefore this
> Sonnet states that, though it is nonexistent for the profane, it
> comes into being as soon as it appears in the "mirror" which
> the virgin holds up in front of it (see the tapestries of the 15th
> century) and "in her," as in a second mirror that is just as pure,
> just as mysterious.
>
> (To Countess Margot Sizzo-Noris-Crouy,
> June 1, 1923)

V (Muzot, February 15, 1922; chronologically the first poem of the Sec-
ond Part)

l. 7, so *overpowered with abundance:*

> I am like the little anemone I once saw in the garden in Rome:
> it had opened so wide during the day that it could no longer
> close at night. It was terrifying to see it in the dark meadow,
> wide open, still taking everything in, into its calyx, which
> seemed as if it had been furiously torn back, with the much
> too vast night above it. And alongside, all its prudent sisters,
> each one closed around its small measure of profusion.
>
> (To Lou Andreas-Salomé, June 26, 1914)

VI (Muzot, February 15, 1922)

> the rose of antiquity was a simple "eglantine," red and yellow, in the colors that appear in flame. It blooms here, in the Valais, in certain gardens.
>
> —Rilke's note

> Every day, as I contemplate these admirable white roses, I wonder whether they aren't the most perfect image of that unity—I would even say, that identity—of absence and presence which perhaps constitutes the fundamental equation of our life.
>
> (To Madame M.-R., January 4, 1923)

VII (Muzot, February 15/17, 1922)

> By the brook I picked marsh-marigolds, almost green, a bit of quite fresh yellow painted into the calyx at the last moment. Inside, around the stamens, an oil-soaked circle, as if they had eaten butter. Green smell from the tubelike stems. Then to find it left behind on my hand, closely related through it. Girl friends, long ago in childhood, with their hot hands: was it this that so moved me?
>
> (Spanish Notebook, 1913; quoted in *Rilke und Benvenuta,* Wien: W. Andermann, 1943, p. 157)

VIII (Muzot, February 15/17, 1922)

l. 4, *the lamb with the talking scroll:*

> The lamb (in medieval paintings) which speaks only by means of a scroll with an inscription on it.
>
> —Rilke's note

Dedication, *Egon von Rilke* (1873–1880): Youngest child of Rilke's father's brother. He also appears in the Fourth Elegy, p. 23.

> I think of him often and keep returning to his image, which has remained indescribably moving to me. So much

"childhood"—the sad and helpless side of childhood—is embodied for me in his form, in the ruff he wore, his little neck, his chin, his beautiful disfigured eyes. So I evoked him once more in connection with that eighth sonnet, which expresses transience, after he had already served, in the Notebooks of Malte Laurids Brigge, as the model for little Erik Brahe, who died in childhood.

> (To Phia Rilke, January 24, 1924; in Carl Sieber, *René Rilke: Die Jugend Rainer Maria Rilkes*, Leipzig: Insel Verlag, 1932, pp. 59 f.)

IX (Muzot, February 15/17, 1922)

X (Muzot, February 15/17, 1922)

XI (Muzot, February 15/17, 1922)

Refers to the way in which, according to an ancient hunting-custom in certain regions of Karst, the strangely pale grotto-doves are caught. Hunters carefully lower large pieces of cloth into the caverns and then suddenly shake them. The doves, frightened out, are shot during their terrified escape.

> —Rilke's note

Meanwhile I went along on a dove-hunting expedition to one of the Karst grottos, quietly eating juniper berries while the hunters forgot me in their concentration on the beautiful wild doves flying with loud wingbeats out of the caves.

> (To Katharina Kippenberg, October 31, 1911)

l. 4, *Karst:* A region along the Dalmatian coast (north of Trieste and not far from Duino Castle) known for its limestone caverns.

XII (Muzot, February 15/17, 1922)

l. 13, *Daphne:* A nymph pursued by Apollo and transformed into a laurel. See Ovid, Metamorphoses I, 452 ff.

XIII (Muzot, February 15/17, 1922)

In a letter telling Vera's mother about the unexpected appearance of the second part of the Sonnets, Rilke wrote:

Today I am sending you only *one* of these sonnets, because, of the entire cycle, it is the one that is closest to me and ultimately the one that is the most valid.

(To Gertrud Ouckama Knoop, March 18, 1922)

The thirteenth sonnet of the second part is for me the most valid of all. It includes all the others, and it expresses *that* which—though it still far exceeds me—my purest, most final achievement would someday, in the midst of life, have to be.

(To Katharina Kippenberg, April 2, 1922)

l. 14, *cancel the count:*

Renunciation of love or fulfillment in love: *both* are wonderful and beyond compare only where the entire love-experience, with *all* its barely differentiable ecstasies, is allowed to occupy a central position: there (in the rapture of a few lovers or saints of *all* times and *all* religions) renunciation and completion are identical. Where the infinite *wholly* enters (whether as minus or plus), the ah so human number drops away, as the road that has now been completely traveled—and what remains is the having arrived, *the being!*

(To Rudolf Bodländer, March 23, 1922)

XIV (Muzot, February 15/17, 1922)

XV (Muzot, February 17, 1922)

XVI (Muzot, February 17/19, 1922)

XVII (Muzot, February 17/19, 1922)

XVIII (Muzot, February 17/19, 1922)

XIX (Muzot, February 17/23, 1922)

XX (Muzot, February 17/23, 1922)

l. 5, *Fate:*

What we call fate does not come into us from the outside, but emerges *from* us.

(To Franz Xaver Kappus, August 12, 1904)

l. 10, *fish:*

. . . I sank, weighted down with a millstone's torpor, to the bottom of silence, below the fish, who only at times pucker their mouths into a discreet Oh, which is inaudible.

(To Princess Marie von Thurn und Taxis-Hohenlohe,
January 14, 1913)

l. 13, *a place:*

Jacobsen once wrote how annoyed he was that his remarkable short novel had to be called "Two Worlds"; again and again he had felt compelled to say: "Two World." In the same way, it often happens that one is at odds with the outward behavior of language and wants something inside it, an innermost language, a language of word-kernels, a language which is not plucked from stems, up above, but gathered as language-seeds—wouldn't the perfect hymn to the sun be composed in this language, and isn't the pure silence of love like heart-soil around such language-kernels? Ah, how often one wishes to speak a few levels deeper; my prose in "Proposal for an Experiment" ["Primal Sound"] lies deeper, gets a bit farther into the essential, than the prose of the *Malte,* but one penetrates such a very little way down, one remains with just an intuition of what kind of speech is possible in the place where silence is.

(To Nanny Wunderly-Volkart, February 4, 1920)

### XXI (Muzot, February 17/23, 1922)

l. 3, *Ispahan* (mod., Isfahan) *or Shiraz:* Persian cities famous for their magnificent gardens. Shiraz also contains the tombs of the poets Hafiz and Sa'di.

### XXII (Muzot, February 17/23, 1922)

l. 5, *bell:*

For me it was Easter just once; that was during the long, excited, extraordinary night when, with the whole populace crowding around, the bells of Ivan Veliky crashed into me in the darkness, one after another. That was my Easter, and I think it is huge enough for a whole lifetime. . . .

(To Lou Andreas-Salomé, March 31, 1904)

l. 7, *Karnak:* See note on p. 235.

### XXIII (Muzot, February 17/23, 1922)

(to the reader)

—Rilke's note

l. 3, *a dog's imploring glance:*

Alas, I have not completely gotten over expecting the "nouvelle opération" to come from some human intervention; and yet, what's the use, since it is my lot to pass the human by, as it were, and arrive at the extreme limit, the edge of the earth, as recently in Cordova, when an ugly little bitch, in the last stage of pregnancy, came up to me. She was not a remarkable animal, was full of accidental puppies over whom no great fuss would be made; but since we were all alone, she came over to me, hard as it was for her, and raised her eyes enlarged by trouble and inwardness and sought my glance—and in her own way was truly everything that goes beyond the individual, to I don't know where, into the future or into the incomprehensible. The situation ended in her getting a lump of sugar from my coffee, but incidentally, oh so incidentally, we read Mass together, so to speak; in itself, the action was nothing but giving and receiving, yet the sense and the seriousness and our whole silent understanding was beyond all bounds.

(To Princess Marie von Thurn und Taxis-Hohenlohe,<br>December 17, 1912)

XXIV (Muzot, February 19/23, 1922)

l. 5, *Gods:*

Does it confuse you that I say God and gods and, for the sake of completeness, haunt you with these dogmatic words (as with a ghost), thinking that they will have some kind of meaning for you also? But grant, for a moment, that there is a realm beyond the senses. Let us agree that from his earliest beginnings man has created gods in whom just the deadly and menacing and destructive and terrifying elements in life were contained—its violence, its fury, its impersonal bewilderment—all tied together into one thick knot of malevolence: something alien to us, if you wish, but something which let us admit that we were aware of it, endured it, even acknowledged it for the sake of a sure, mysterious relationship and inclusion in it. For *we were this too;* only we didn't know what to do with this side of our experience; it was too large, too dangerous, too many-sided, it grew above and beyond us, into an excess of meaning; we found it impossible (what with the many demands of a life adapted to habit and achievement) to deal with these unwieldly and ungraspable forces; and so we agreed to place them outside us.—But since they were an overflow of our own being, its most powerful element, indeed were *too* powerful, were huge, violent, incomprehensible, often monstrous—: how could they not, concentrated in one place, exert an influence and ascendancy over us? And, remember, from the outside now. Couldn't the history of God be treated as an almost never-explored area of the human soul, one that has always been postponed, saved, and finally neglected . . . ?

And then, you see, the same thing happened with death. Experienced, yet not to be fully experienced by us in its reality, continually overshadowing us yet never truly acknowledged, forever violating and surpassing the meaning of life—it too was banished and expelled, so that it might not constantly interrupt us in the search for this meaning. Death, which is probably so close to us that the distance between it and the life-center inside us cannot be measured, now became something external, held farther away from us every day, a presence that lurked somewhere in the void, ready to pounce upon this person or that in its evil choice. More and more, the suspicion grew up against death that it was the contradiction, the adversary, the invisible opposite in the air, the force that makes all our joys wither, the perilous glass of our happiness, out of which we may be spilled at any moment. . . .

All this might still have made a kind of sense if we had been able to keep God and death at a distance, as mere ideas in the realm of the mind—: but Nature knew nothing of this banishment that we had somehow accomplished—when a tree blossoms, death as well as life blossoms in it, and the field is full of death, which from its reclining face sends forth a rich expression of life, and the animals move patiently from one to the other—and everywhere around us, death is at home, and it watches us out of the cracks in Things, and a rusty nail that sticks out of a plank somewhere, does nothing day and night except rejoice over death.

(To Lotte Hepner, November 8, 1915)

XXV (Muzot, February 19/23, 1922)

(Companion-piece to the first spring-song of the children in
the First Part of the Sonnets)

—Rilke's note

XXVI (Muzot, February 19/23, 1922)

XXVII (Muzot, February 19/23, 1922)

l. 4, *Demiurge:* In the Gnostic tradition, a lower deity who created the
world of time.

XXVIII (Muzot, February 19/23, 1922)

(to Vera)

—Rilke's note

XXIX (Muzot, February 19/23, 1922)

(to a friend of Vera's)

—Rilke's note

l. 3, *like a bell:*

With this bell tower the little island, in all its fervor, is
attached to the past; the tower fixes the dates and dissolves
them again, because ever since it was built it has been ringing
out time and destiny over the lake, as though it included in
itself the visibility of all the lives that have been surrendered
here; as though again and again it were sending their transi-
toriness into space, invisibly, in the sonorous transformations
of its notes.

(To Countess Aline Dietrichstein, June 26, 1917)

l. 4, *What feeds upon your face:*

> Oh and the night, the night, when the wind full of cosmic
> space / feeds upon our face—
>
> (The First Elegy, ll. 18 f.)

Breathe-in the darkness of earth and again
look up! Again. Airy and faceless,
from above, the depths bend toward you. The face that is dis-
solved
and contained in the night will give more space to your own.
  ("Overflowing heavens of lavished stars," in *Ahead of All Parting*,
Modern Library, 1995, p. 117)

l. 10, *in their magic ring:*

> [The poet's] is a naïve, aeolian soul, which is not ashamed to
> dwell where the senses intersect [*sich kreuzen*], and which lacks
> nothing, because these unfolded senses form a ring in which
> there are no gaps.
>
> ("The Books of a Woman in Love," SW 6, 1018)

## APPENDIX TO THE SONNETS TO ORPHEUS

> My dear, hardly had Strohl sent me back the little book
> with the 25 Orpheus Sonnets when this thread proceeded
> further, into a new fabric—a quantity of additional Son-
> nets have arisen these past few days, perhaps fifteen or more,
> but I won't keep them all—I am now so rich that I can afford to
> *choose*! What a world of grace we live in, after all! What powers
> are waiting to fill us, constantly shaken vessels that we are. We
> think we are under one kind of "guidance"—but they are
> already at work *inside* us. The only thing that belongs to us, as
> completely ours, is patience; but what immense capital that
> is—and what interest it bears in its time!—Consolation
> enough for eighthundredthirtyseven lives of average length.
>
> (To Nanny Wunderly-Volkart, February 18, 1922)

[I] (Muzot, approximately February 3, 1922; first version of Sonnet VII, First Part)

> And I would appreciate it if you could *replace* the VIIth Sonnet with the enclosed variant (just the first stanza of the previous version remains—the rest always embarrassed me by its exaggerated pathos, and I have long since crossed it out).
>
> (To Gertrud Ouckama Knoop, March 18, 1922)

l. 14, *Golden Fleece:* In some versions of the myth, Orpheus accompanied Jason and the Argonauts on their voyage.

[II] (Muzot, February 2/5, 1922; originally Sonnet XXI, First Part)

[III] (Muzot, February 15/17, 1922)

[IV] (Muzot, February 15/17, 1922)

l. 1, *stela:* cf. the Second Elegy, ll. 66 ff., and the notes on p. 228.

[V] (Muzot, February 16/17, 1922)

This Sonnet probably refers to Goethe, who at the age of seventy-four fell in love with the nineteen-year-old Ulrike von Levetzow.

l. 9, *Hymen:* Greek god of marriage, usually depicted as a handsome young man crowned with a wreath and holding a wedding-torch.

l. 12, *laments:* Goethe commemorated his love in a poem known as the Marienbad Elegy.

[VI] (Muzot, February 16/17, 1922)

l. 3, *Villa d'Este:* Italian Renaissance palace near Tivoli, famous for its fountains and terraced gardens.

[VII] (Muzot, February 16/17, 1922)

[VIII] (Muzot, February 17/19, 1922)

[IX] (Muzot, approximately February 23, 1922)

FRAGMENTS

[i] (Muzot, approximately February 3; written between Sonnets VIII and IX, First Part)

[ii] (Muzot, approximately February 3, 1922; related to Sonnet XI, First Part)

[iii] (Muzot, approximately February 4, 1922; written between Sonnets XVII and XVIII, First Part)

[iv] (Muzot, February 12 or 13, 1922; draft of Sonnet II, Second Part)

[v] (Muzot, February 16/17, 1922)

[vi] (Muzot, February 16/17, 1922)

[vii] (Muzot, February 17/19, 1922)

[viii] (Muzot, February 19/23, 1922; draft of Sonnet XXV, Second Part)

[ix] (Muzot, February 19/23, 1922)

[x] (Muzot, approximately February 23, 1922)

[xi] (Muzot, approximately February 23, 1922)

# Acknowledgments

I would like to thank Michael André Bernstein, Chana Bloch, Jonathan Galassi (my editor at Random House), John Herman (my editor at Simon & Schuster), W. S. Merwin, Robert Pinsky, and Alan Williamson for their many helpful suggestions.

I owe a great deal to Robert Hass for his brilliant essay "Looking for Rilke," which was the introduction to *The Selected Poetry* and was later included in his *Twentieth Century Pleasures.*

During the months when I was studying the *Elegies*, I lived in close daily contact with Jacob Steiner's great line-by-line commentary, *Rilkes Duineser Elegien*, and found it an almost never-failing source of illumination.

Finally, I must acknowledge my debt to the work of J. B. Leishman, M. D. Herter Norton, and C. F. MacIntyre, to the Young, Boney, Guerne, and Gaspar version of the *Elegies*, and to the Poulin *Elegies and Sonnets.*

And to Vicki Chang: inexpressible love and gratitude.

# Index of Titles and First Lines

## (German)

# Index of Titles and First Lines

## (English)